C-3177  CAREER EXAMINATION SERIES

*This is your*
*PASSBOOK for...*

# Sanitation Enforcement Agent

*Test Preparation Study Guide*
*Questions & Answers*

NATIONAL LEARNING CORPORATION®

# COPYRIGHT NOTICE

This book is SOLELY intended for, is sold ONLY to, and its use is RESTRICTED to individual, bona fide applicants or candidates who qualify by virtue of having seriously filed applications for appropriate license, certificate, professional and/or promotional advancement, higher school matriculation, scholarship, or other legitimate requirements of education and/or governmental authorities.

This book is NOT intended for use, class instruction, tutoring, training, duplication, copying, reprinting, excerption, or adaptation, etc., by:

1) Other publishers
2) Proprietors and/or Instructors of "Coaching" and/or Preparatory Courses
3) Personnel and/or Training Divisions of commercial, industrial, and governmental organizations
4) Schools, colleges, or universities and/or their departments and staffs, including teachers and other personnel
5) Testing Agencies or Bureaus
6) Study groups which seek by the purchase of a single volume to copy and/or duplicate and/or adapt this material for use by the group as a whole without having purchased individual volumes for each of the members of the group
7) Et al.

Such persons would be in violation of appropriate Federal and State statutes.

PROVISION OF LICENSING AGREEMENTS – Recognized educational, commercial, industrial, and governmental institutions and organizations, and others legitimately engaged in educational pursuits, including training, testing, and measurement activities, may address request for a licensing agreement to the copyright owners, who will determine whether, and under what conditions, including fees and charges, the materials in this book may be used them. In other words, a licensing facility exists for the legitimate use of the material in this book on other than an individual basis. However, it is asseverated and affirmed here that the material in this book CANNOT be used without the receipt of the express permission of such a licensing agreement from the Publishers. Inquiries re licensing should be addressed to the company, attention rights and permissions department.

All rights reserved, including the right of reproduction in whole or in part, in any form or by any means, electronic or mechanical, including photocopying, recording, or by any information storage and retrieval system, without permission in writing from the Publisher.

Copyright © 2024 by
## National Learning Corporation

212 Michael Drive, Syosset, NY 11791
(516) 921-8888 • www.passbooks.com
E-mail: info@passbooks.com

PUBLISHED IN THE UNITED STATES OF AMERICA

# PASSBOOK® SERIES

THE *PASSBOOK® SERIES* has been created to prepare applicants and candidates for the ultimate academic battlefield – the examination room.

At some time in our lives, each and every one of us may be required to take an examination – for validation, matriculation, admission, qualification, registration, certification, or licensure.

Based on the assumption that every applicant or candidate has met the basic formal educational standards, has taken the required number of courses, and read the necessary texts, the *PASSBOOK® SERIES* furnishes the one special preparation which may assure passing with confidence, instead of failing with insecurity. Examination questions – together with answers – are furnished as the basic vehicle for study so that the mysteries of the examination and its compounding difficulties may be eliminated or diminished by a sure method.

This book is meant to help you pass your examination provided that you qualify and are serious in your objective.

The entire field is reviewed through the huge store of content information which is succinctly presented through a provocative and challenging approach – the question-and-answer method.

A climate of success is established by furnishing the correct answers at the end of each test.

You soon learn to recognize types of questions, forms of questions, and patterns of questioning. You may even begin to anticipate expected outcomes.

You perceive that many questions are repeated or adapted so that you can gain acute insights, which may enable you to score many sure points.

You learn how to confront new questions, or types of questions, and to attack them confidently and work out the correct answers.

You note objectives and emphases, and recognize pitfalls and dangers, so that you may make positive educational adjustments.

Moreover, you are kept fully informed in relation to new concepts, methods, practices, and directions in the field.

You discover that you are actually taking the examination all the time: you are preparing for the examination by "taking" an examination, not by reading extraneous and/or supererogatory textbooks.

In short, this PASSBOOK®, used directedly, should be an important factor in helping you to pass your test.

# SANITATION ENFORCEMENT AGENT

## DUTIES
Under supervision, the Sanitation Enforcement Agent is responsible for the enforcement of certain laws, rules and regulations of the health and administrative codes, state public health law, state vehicle and traffic laws, and traffic regulations; prepares and issues summonses for certain violations thereof; performs security duty at department of sanitation facilities; performs related work.

## SCOPE OF THE EXAMINATION
The multiple-choice test may include questions on remembering new information; understanding the order in which to do things; understanding written language; communicating information to another person; recognizing the existence of a problem; applying general rules to a specific situation or identifying a common element in several different situations; recognizing where you are in relation to the space you are in and using a map or diagram to get from one position to another; and other related areas.

# HOW TO TAKE A TEST

I. YOU MUST PASS AN EXAMINATION

A. *WHAT EVERY CANDIDATE SHOULD KNOW*

Examination applicants often ask us for help in preparing for the written test. What can I study in advance? What kinds of questions will be asked? How will the test be given? How will the papers be graded?

As an applicant for a civil service examination, you may be wondering about some of these things. Our purpose here is to suggest effective methods of advance study and to describe civil service examinations.

Your chances for success on this examination can be increased if you know how to prepare. Those "pre-examination jitters" can be reduced if you know what to expect. You can even experience an adventure in good citizenship if you know why civil service exams are given.

B. *WHY ARE CIVIL SERVICE EXAMINATIONS GIVEN?*

Civil service examinations are important to you in two ways. As a citizen, you want public jobs filled by employees who know how to do their work. As a job seeker, you want a fair chance to compete for that job on an equal footing with other candidates. The best-known means of accomplishing this two-fold goal is the competitive examination.

Exams are widely publicized throughout the nation. They may be administered for jobs in federal, state, city, municipal, town or village governments or agencies.

Any citizen may apply, with some limitations, such as the age or residence of applicants. Your experience and education may be reviewed to see whether you meet the requirements for the particular examination. When these requirements exist, they are reasonable and applied consistently to all applicants. Thus, a competitive examination may cause you some uneasiness now, but it is your privilege and safeguard.

C. *HOW ARE CIVIL SERVICE EXAMS DEVELOPED?*

Examinations are carefully written by trained technicians who are specialists in the field known as "psychological measurement," in consultation with recognized authorities in the field of work that the test will cover. These experts recommend the subject matter areas or skills to be tested; only those knowledges or skills important to your success on the job are included. The most reliable books and source materials available are used as references. Together, the experts and technicians judge the difficulty level of the questions.

Test technicians know how to phrase questions so that the problem is clearly stated. Their ethics do not permit "trick" or "catch" questions. Questions may have been tried out on sample groups, or subjected to statistical analysis, to determine their usefulness.

Written tests are often used in combination with performance tests, ratings of training and experience, and oral interviews. All of these measures combine to form the best-known means of finding the right person for the right job.

## II. HOW TO PASS THE WRITTEN TEST

### A. NATURE OF THE EXAMINATION

To prepare intelligently for civil service examinations, you should know how they differ from school examinations you have taken. In school you were assigned certain definite pages to read or subjects to cover. The examination questions were quite detailed and usually emphasized memory. Civil service exams, on the other hand, try to discover your present ability to perform the duties of a position, plus your potentiality to learn these duties. In other words, a civil service exam attempts to predict how successful you will be. Questions cover such a broad area that they cannot be as minute and detailed as school exam questions.

In the public service similar kinds of work, or positions, are grouped together in one "class." This process is known as *position-classification*. All the positions in a class are paid according to the salary range for that class. One class title covers all of these positions, and they are all tested by the same examination.

### B. FOUR BASIC STEPS

#### 1) Study the announcement

How, then, can you know what subjects to study? Our best answer is: "Learn as much as possible about the class of positions for which you've applied." The exam will test the knowledge, skills and abilities needed to do the work.

Your most valuable source of information about the position you want is the official exam announcement. This announcement lists the training and experience qualifications. Check these standards and apply only if you come reasonably close to meeting them.

The brief description of the position in the examination announcement offers some clues to the subjects which will be tested. Think about the job itself. Review the duties in your mind. Can you perform them, or are there some in which you are rusty? Fill in the blank spots in your preparation.

Many jurisdictions preview the written test in the exam announcement by including a section called "Knowledge and Abilities Required," "Scope of the Examination," or some similar heading. Here you will find out specifically what fields will be tested.

#### 2) Review your own background

Once you learn in general what the position is all about, and what you need to know to do the work, ask yourself which subjects you already know fairly well and which need improvement. You may wonder whether to concentrate on improving your strong areas or on building some background in your fields of weakness. When the announcement has specified "some knowledge" or "considerable knowledge," or has used adjectives like "beginning principles of…" or "advanced … methods," you can get a clue as to the number and difficulty of questions to be asked in any given field. More questions, and hence broader coverage, would be included for those subjects which are more important in the work. Now weigh your strengths and weaknesses against the job requirements and prepare accordingly.

#### 3) Determine the level of the position

Another way to tell how intensively you should prepare is to understand the level of the job for which you are applying. Is it the entering level? In other words, is this the position in which beginners in a field of work are hired? Or is it an intermediate or advanced level? Sometimes this is indicated by such words as "Junior" or "Senior" in the class title. Other jurisdictions use Roman numerals to designate the level – Clerk I, Clerk II, for example. The word "Supervisor" sometimes appears in the title. If the level is not indicated by the title, check the description of duties. Will you be working under very close supervision, or will you have responsibility for independent decisions in this work?

### 4) Choose appropriate study materials

Now that you know the subjects to be examined and the relative amount of each subject to be covered, you can choose suitable study materials. For beginning level jobs, or even advanced ones, if you have a pronounced weakness in some aspect of your training, read a modern, standard textbook in that field. Be sure it is up to date and has general coverage. Such books are normally available at your library, and the librarian will be glad to help you locate one. For entry-level positions, questions of appropriate difficulty are chosen – neither highly advanced questions, nor those too simple. Such questions require careful thought but not advanced training.

If the position for which you are applying is technical or advanced, you will read more advanced, specialized material. If you are already familiar with the basic principles of your field, elementary textbooks would waste your time. Concentrate on advanced textbooks and technical periodicals. Think through the concepts and review difficult problems in your field.

These are all general sources. You can get more ideas on your own initiative, following these leads. For example, training manuals and publications of the government agency which employs workers in your field can be useful, particularly for technical and professional positions. A letter or visit to the government department involved may result in more specific study suggestions, and certainly will provide you with a more definite idea of the exact nature of the position you are seeking.

## III. KINDS OF TESTS

Tests are used for purposes other than measuring knowledge and ability to perform specified duties. For some positions, it is equally important to test ability to make adjustments to new situations or to profit from training. In others, basic mental abilities not dependent on information are essential. Questions which test these things may not appear as pertinent to the duties of the position as those which test for knowledge and information. Yet they are often highly important parts of a fair examination. For very general questions, it is almost impossible to help you direct your study efforts. What we can do is to point out some of the more common of these general abilities needed in public service positions and describe some typical questions.

1) General information

Broad, general information has been found useful for predicting job success in some kinds of work. This is tested in a variety of ways, from vocabulary lists to questions about current events. Basic background in some field of work, such as sociology or economics, may be sampled in a group of questions. Often these are principles which have become familiar to most persons through exposure rather than through formal training. It is difficult to advise you how to study for these questions; being alert to the world around you is our best suggestion.

2) Verbal ability

An example of an ability needed in many positions is verbal or language ability. Verbal ability is, in brief, the ability to use and understand words. Vocabulary and grammar tests are typical measures of this ability. Reading comprehension or paragraph interpretation questions are common in many kinds of civil service tests. You are given a paragraph of written material and asked to find its central meaning.

### 3) Numerical ability

Number skills can be tested by the familiar arithmetic problem, by checking paired lists of numbers to see which are alike and which are different, or by interpreting charts and graphs. In the latter test, a graph may be printed in the test booklet which you are asked to use as the basis for answering questions.

### 4) Observation

A popular test for law-enforcement positions is the observation test. A picture is shown to you for several minutes, then taken away. Questions about the picture test your ability to observe both details and larger elements.

### 5) Following directions

In many positions in the public service, the employee must be able to carry out written instructions dependably and accurately. You may be given a chart with several columns, each column listing a variety of information. The questions require you to carry out directions involving the information given in the chart.

### 6) Skills and aptitudes

Performance tests effectively measure some manual skills and aptitudes. When the skill is one in which you are trained, such as typing or shorthand, you can practice. These tests are often very much like those given in business school or high school courses. For many of the other skills and aptitudes, however, no short-time preparation can be made. Skills and abilities natural to you or that you have developed throughout your lifetime are being tested.

Many of the general questions just described provide all the data needed to answer the questions and ask you to use your reasoning ability to find the answers. Your best preparation for these tests, as well as for tests of facts and ideas, is to be at your physical and mental best. You, no doubt, have your own methods of getting into an exam-taking mood and keeping "in shape." The next section lists some ideas on this subject.


## IV. KINDS OF QUESTIONS

Only rarely is the "essay" question, which you answer in narrative form, used in civil service tests. Civil service tests are usually of the short-answer type. Full instructions for answering these questions will be given to you at the examination. But in case this is your first experience with short-answer questions and separate answer sheets, here is what you need to know:

### 1) Multiple-choice Questions

Most popular of the short-answer questions is the "multiple choice" or "best answer" question. It can be used, for example, to test for factual knowledge, ability to solve problems or judgment in meeting situations found at work.

A multiple-choice question is normally one of three types—
- It can begin with an incomplete statement followed by several possible endings. You are to find the one ending which *best* completes the statement, although some of the others may not be entirely wrong.
- It can also be a complete statement in the form of a question which is answered by choosing one of the statements listed.

- It can be in the form of a problem – again you select the best answer.

Here is an example of a multiple-choice question with a discussion which should give you some clues as to the method for choosing the right answer:

When an employee has a complaint about his assignment, the action which will *best* help him overcome his difficulty is to
    A. discuss his difficulty with his coworkers
    B. take the problem to the head of the organization
    C. take the problem to the person who gave him the assignment
    D. say nothing to anyone about his complaint

In answering this question, you should study each of the choices to find which is best. Consider choice "A" – Certainly an employee may discuss his complaint with fellow employees, but no change or improvement can result, and the complaint remains unresolved. Choice "B" is a poor choice since the head of the organization probably does not know what assignment you have been given, and taking your problem to him is known as "going over the head" of the supervisor. The supervisor, or person who made the assignment, is the person who can clarify it or correct any injustice. Choice "C" is, therefore, correct. To say nothing, as in choice "D," is unwise. Supervisors have and interest in knowing the problems employees are facing, and the employee is seeking a solution to his problem.

### 2) True/False Questions

The "true/false" or "right/wrong" form of question is sometimes used. Here a complete statement is given. Your job is to decide whether the statement is right or wrong.

SAMPLE: A roaming cell-phone call to a nearby city costs less than a non-roaming call to a distant city.

This statement is wrong, or false, since roaming calls are more expensive.

This is not a complete list of all possible question forms, although most of the others are variations of these common types. You will always get complete directions for answering questions. Be sure you understand *how* to mark your answers – ask questions until you do.

### V. RECORDING YOUR ANSWERS

Computer terminals are used more and more today for many different kinds of exams.

For an examination with very few applicants, you may be told to record your answers in the test booklet itself. Separate answer sheets are much more common. If this separate answer sheet is to be scored by machine – and this is often the case – it is highly important that you mark your answers correctly in order to get credit.

An electronic scoring machine is often used in civil service offices because of the speed with which papers can be scored. Machine-scored answer sheets must be marked with a pencil, which will be given to you. This pencil has a high graphite content which responds to the electronic scoring machine. As a matter of fact, stray dots may register as answers, so do not let your pencil rest on the answer sheet while you are pondering the correct answer. Also, if your pencil lead breaks or is otherwise defective, ask for another.

Since the answer sheet will be dropped in a slot in the scoring machine, be careful not to bend the corners or get the paper crumpled.

The answer sheet normally has five vertical columns of numbers, with 30 numbers to a column. These numbers correspond to the question numbers in your test booklet. After each number, going across the page are four or five pairs of dotted lines. These short dotted lines have small letters or numbers above them. The first two pairs may also have a "T" or "F" above the letters. This indicates that the first two pairs only are to be used if the questions are of the true-false type. If the questions are multiple choice, disregard the "T" and "F" and pay attention only to the small letters or numbers.

Answer your questions in the manner of the sample that follows:

32. The largest city in the United States is
    A. Washington, D.C.
    B. New York City
    C. Chicago
    D. Detroit
    E. San Francisco

1) Choose the answer you think is best. (New York City is the largest, so "B" is correct.)
2) Find the row of dotted lines numbered the same as the question you are answering. (Find row number 32)
3) Find the pair of dotted lines corresponding to the answer. (Find the pair of lines under the mark "B.")
4) Make a solid black mark between the dotted lines.

## VI. BEFORE THE TEST

Common sense will help you find procedures to follow to get ready for an examination. Too many of us, however, overlook these sensible measures. Indeed, nervousness and fatigue have been found to be the most serious reasons why applicants fail to do their best on civil service tests. Here is a list of reminders:

- Begin your preparation early – Don't wait until the last minute to go scurrying around for books and materials or to find out what the position is all about.
- Prepare continuously – An hour a night for a week is better than an all-night cram session. This has been definitely established. What is more, a night a week for a month will return better dividends than crowding your study into a shorter period of time.
- Locate the place of the exam – You have been sent a notice telling you when and where to report for the examination. If the location is in a different town or otherwise unfamiliar to you, it would be well to inquire the best route and learn something about the building.
- Relax the night before the test – Allow your mind to rest. Do not study at all that night. Plan some mild recreation or diversion; then go to bed early and get a good night's sleep.
- Get up early enough to make a leisurely trip to the place for the test – This way unforeseen events, traffic snarls, unfamiliar buildings, etc. will not upset you.
- Dress comfortably – A written test is not a fashion show. You will be known by number and not by name, so wear something comfortable.

- Leave excess paraphernalia at home – Shopping bags and odd bundles will get in your way. You need bring only the items mentioned in the official notice you received; usually everything you need is provided. Do not bring reference books to the exam. They will only confuse those last minutes and be taken away from you when in the test room.
- Arrive somewhat ahead of time – If because of transportation schedules you must get there very early, bring a newspaper or magazine to take your mind off yourself while waiting.
- Locate the examination room – When you have found the proper room, you will be directed to the seat or part of the room where you will sit. Sometimes you are given a sheet of instructions to read while you are waiting. Do not fill out any forms until you are told to do so; just read them and be prepared.
- Relax and prepare to listen to the instructions
- If you have any physical problem that may keep you from doing your best, be sure to tell the test administrator. If you are sick or in poor health, you really cannot do your best on the exam. You can come back and take the test some other time.

## VII. AT THE TEST

The day of the test is here and you have the test booklet in your hand. The temptation to get going is very strong. Caution! There is more to success than knowing the right answers. You must know how to identify your papers and understand variations in the type of short-answer question used in this particular examination. Follow these suggestions for maximum results from your efforts:

### 1) Cooperate with the monitor

The test administrator has a duty to create a situation in which you can be as much at ease as possible. He will give instructions, tell you when to begin, check to see that you are marking your answer sheet correctly, and so on. He is not there to guard you, although he will see that your competitors do not take unfair advantage. He wants to help you do your best.

### 2) Listen to all instructions

Don't jump the gun! Wait until you understand all directions. In most civil service tests you get more time than you need to answer the questions. So don't be in a hurry. Read each word of instructions until you clearly understand the meaning. Study the examples, listen to all announcements and follow directions. Ask questions if you do not understand what to do.

### 3) Identify your papers

Civil service exams are usually identified by number only. You will be assigned a number; you must not put your name on your test papers. Be sure to copy your number correctly. Since more than one exam may be given, copy your exact examination title.

### 4) Plan your time

Unless you are told that a test is a "speed" or "rate of work" test, speed itself is usually not important. Time enough to answer all the questions will be provided, but this does not mean that you have all day. An overall time limit has been set. Divide the total time (in minutes) by the number of questions to determine the approximate time you have for each question.

**5) Do not linger over difficult questions**

If you come across a difficult question, mark it with a paper clip (useful to have along) and come back to it when you have been through the booklet. One caution if you do this – be sure to skip a number on your answer sheet as well. Check often to be sure that you have not lost your place and that you are marking in the row numbered the same as the question you are answering.

**6) Read the questions**

Be sure you know what the question asks! Many capable people are unsuccessful because they failed to *read* the questions correctly.

**7) Answer all questions**

Unless you have been instructed that a penalty will be deducted for incorrect answers, it is better to guess than to omit a question.

**8) Speed tests**

It is often better NOT to guess on speed tests. It has been found that on timed tests people are tempted to spend the last few seconds before time is called in marking answers at random – without even reading them – in the hope of picking up a few extra points. To discourage this practice, the instructions may warn you that your score will be "corrected" for guessing. That is, a penalty will be applied. The incorrect answers will be deducted from the correct ones, or some other penalty formula will be used.

**9) Review your answers**

If you finish before time is called, go back to the questions you guessed or omitted to give them further thought. Review other answers if you have time.

**10) Return your test materials**

If you are ready to leave before others have finished or time is called, take ALL your materials to the monitor and leave quietly. Never take any test material with you. The monitor can discover whose papers are not complete, and taking a test booklet may be grounds for disqualification.

## VIII. EXAMINATION TECHNIQUES

1) Read the general instructions carefully. These are usually printed on the first page of the exam booklet. As a rule, these instructions refer to the timing of the examination; the fact that you should not start work until the signal and must stop work at a signal, etc. If there are any *special* instructions, such as a choice of questions to be answered, make sure that you note this instruction carefully.

2) When you are ready to start work on the examination, that is as soon as the signal has been given, read the instructions to each question booklet, underline any key words or phrases, such as *least, best, outline, describe* and the like. In this way you will tend to answer as requested rather than discover on reviewing your paper that you *listed without describing*, that you selected the *worst* choice rather than the *best* choice, etc.

3) If the examination is of the objective or multiple-choice type – that is, each question will also give a series of possible answers: A, B, C or D, and you are called upon to select the best answer and write the letter next to that answer on your answer paper – it is advisable to start answering each question in turn. There may be anywhere from 50 to 100 such questions in the three or four hours allotted and you can see how much time would be taken if you read through all the questions before beginning to answer any. Furthermore, if you come across a question or group of questions which you know would be difficult to answer, it would undoubtedly affect your handling of all the other questions.

4) If the examination is of the essay type and contains but a few questions, it is a moot point as to whether you should read all the questions before starting to answer any one. Of course, if you are given a choice – say five out of seven and the like – then it is essential to read all the questions so you can eliminate the two that are most difficult. If, however, you are asked to answer all the questions, there may be danger in trying to answer the easiest one first because you may find that you will spend too much time on it. The best technique is to answer the first question, then proceed to the second, etc.

5) Time your answers. Before the exam begins, write down the time it started, then add the time allowed for the examination and write down the time it must be completed, then divide the time available somewhat as follows:
    - If 3-1/2 hours are allowed, that would be 210 minutes. If you have 80 objective-type questions, that would be an average of 2-1/2 minutes per question. Allow yourself no more than 2 minutes per question, or a total of 160 minutes, which will permit about 50 minutes to review.
    - If for the time allotment of 210 minutes there are 7 essay questions to answer, that would average about 30 minutes a question. Give yourself only 25 minutes per question so that you have about 35 minutes to review.

6) The most important instruction is to *read each question* and make sure you know what is wanted. The second most important instruction is to *time yourself properly* so that you answer every question. The third most important instruction is to *answer every question*. Guess if you have to but include something for each question. Remember that you will receive no credit for a blank and will probably receive some credit if you write something in answer to an essay question. If you guess a letter – say "B" for a multiple-choice question – you may have guessed right. If you leave a blank as an answer to a multiple-choice question, the examiners may respect your feelings but it will not add a point to your score. Some exams may penalize you for wrong answers, so in such cases *only*, you may not want to guess unless you have some basis for your answer.

7) Suggestions
    a. Objective-type questions
        1. Examine the question booklet for proper sequence of pages and questions
        2. Read all instructions carefully
        3. Skip any question which seems too difficult; return to it after all other questions have been answered
        4. Apportion your time properly; do not spend too much time on any single question or group of questions

5. Note and underline key words – *all, most, fewest, least, best, worst, same, opposite,* etc.
6. Pay particular attention to negatives
7. Note unusual option, e.g., unduly long, short, complex, different or similar in content to the body of the question
8. Observe the use of "hedging" words – *probably, may, most likely,* etc.
9. Make sure that your answer is put next to the same number as the question
10. Do not second-guess unless you have good reason to believe the second answer is definitely more correct
11. Cross out original answer if you decide another answer is more accurate; do not erase until you are ready to hand your paper in
12. Answer all questions; guess unless instructed otherwise
13. Leave time for review

   b. Essay questions
1. Read each question carefully
2. Determine exactly what is wanted. Underline key words or phrases.
3. Decide on outline or paragraph answer
4. Include many different points and elements unless asked to develop any one or two points or elements
5. Show impartiality by giving pros and cons unless directed to select one side only
6. Make and write down any assumptions you find necessary to answer the questions
7. Watch your English, grammar, punctuation and choice of words
8. Time your answers; don't crowd material

8) Answering the essay question

Most essay questions can be answered by framing the specific response around several key words or ideas. Here are a few such key words or ideas:

M's: manpower, materials, methods, money, management
P's: purpose, program, policy, plan, procedure, practice, problems, pitfalls, personnel, public relations

   a. Six basic steps in handling problems:
1. Preliminary plan and background development
2. Collect information, data and facts
3. Analyze and interpret information, data and facts
4. Analyze and develop solutions as well as make recommendations
5. Prepare report and sell recommendations
6. Install recommendations and follow up effectiveness

   b. Pitfalls to avoid
1. *Taking things for granted* – A statement of the situation does not necessarily imply that each of the elements is necessarily true; for example, a complaint may be invalid and biased so that all that can be taken for granted is that a complaint has been registered

2. *Considering only one side of a situation* – Wherever possible, indicate several alternatives and then point out the reasons you selected the best one
3. *Failing to indicate follow up* – Whenever your answer indicates action on your part, make certain that you will take proper follow-up action to see how successful your recommendations, procedures or actions turn out to be
4. *Taking too long in answering any single question* – Remember to time your answers properly

## IX. AFTER THE TEST

Scoring procedures differ in detail among civil service jurisdictions although the general principles are the same. Whether the papers are hand-scored or graded by machine we have described, they are nearly always graded by number. That is, the person who marks the paper knows only the number – never the name – of the applicant. Not until all the papers have been graded will they be matched with names. If other tests, such as training and experience or oral interview ratings have been given, scores will be combined. Different parts of the examination usually have different weights. For example, the written test might count 60 percent of the final grade, and a rating of training and experience 40 percent. In many jurisdictions, veterans will have a certain number of points added to their grades.

After the final grade has been determined, the names are placed in grade order and an eligible list is established. There are various methods for resolving ties between those who get the same final grade – probably the most common is to place first the name of the person whose application was received first. Job offers are made from the eligible list in the order the names appear on it. You will be notified of your grade and your rank as soon as all these computations have been made. This will be done as rapidly as possible.

People who are found to meet the requirements in the announcement are called "eligibles." Their names are put on a list of eligible candidates. An eligible's chances of getting a job depend on how high he stands on this list and how fast agencies are filling jobs from the list.

When a job is to be filled from a list of eligibles, the agency asks for the names of people on the list of eligibles for that job. When the civil service commission receives this request, it sends to the agency the names of the three people highest on this list. Or, if the job to be filled has specialized requirements, the office sends the agency the names of the top three persons who meet these requirements from the general list.

The appointing officer makes a choice from among the three people whose names were sent to him. If the selected person accepts the appointment, the names of the others are put back on the list to be considered for future openings.

That is the rule in hiring from all kinds of eligible lists, whether they are for typist, carpenter, chemist, or something else. For every vacancy, the appointing officer has his choice of any one of the top three eligibles on the list. This explains why the person whose name is on top of the list sometimes does not get an appointment when some of the persons lower on the list do. If the appointing officer chooses the second or third eligible, the No. 1 eligible does not get a job at once, but stays on the list until he is appointed or the list is terminated.

## X. HOW TO PASS THE INTERVIEW TEST

The examination for which you applied requires an oral interview test. You have already taken the written test and you are now being called for the interview test – the final part of the formal examination.

You may think that it is not possible to prepare for an interview test and that there are no procedures to follow during an interview. Our purpose is to point out some things you can do in advance that will help you and some good rules to follow and pitfalls to avoid while you are being interviewed.

*What is an interview supposed to test?*

The written examination is designed to test the technical knowledge and competence of the candidate; the oral is designed to evaluate intangible qualities, not readily measured otherwise, and to establish a list showing the relative fitness of each candidate – as measured against his competitors – for the position sought. Scoring is not on the basis of "right" and "wrong," but on a sliding scale of values ranging from "not passable" to "outstanding." As a matter of fact, it is possible to achieve a relatively low score without a single "incorrect" answer because of evident weakness in the qualities being measured.

Occasionally, an examination may consist entirely of an oral test – either an individual or a group oral. In such cases, information is sought concerning the technical knowledges and abilities of the candidate, since there has been no written examination for this purpose. More commonly, however, an oral test is used to supplement a written examination.

*Who conducts interviews?*

The composition of oral boards varies among different jurisdictions. In nearly all, a representative of the personnel department serves as chairman. One of the members of the board may be a representative of the department in which the candidate would work. In some cases, "outside experts" are used, and, frequently, a businessman or some other representative of the general public is asked to serve. Labor and management or other special groups may be represented. The aim is to secure the services of experts in the appropriate field.

However the board is composed, it is a good idea (and not at all improper or unethical) to ascertain in advance of the interview who the members are and what groups they represent. When you are introduced to them, you will have some idea of their backgrounds and interests, and at least you will not stutter and stammer over their names.

*What should be done before the interview?*

While knowledge about the board members is useful and takes some of the surprise element out of the interview, there is other preparation which is more substantive. It *is* possible to prepare for an oral interview – in several ways:

**1) Keep a copy of your application and review it carefully before the interview**

This may be the only document before the oral board, and the starting point of the interview. Know what education and experience you have listed there, and the sequence and dates of all of it. Sometimes the board will ask you to review the highlights of your experience for them; you should not have to hem and haw doing it.

**2) Study the class specification and the examination announcement**

Usually, the oral board has one or both of these to guide them. The qualities, characteristics or knowledges required by the position sought are stated in these documents. They offer valuable clues as to the nature of the oral interview. For example, if the job involves supervisory responsibilities, the announcement will usually indicate that knowledge of modern supervisory methods and the qualifications of the candidate as a supervisor will be tested. If so, you can expect such questions, frequently in the form of a hypothetical situation which you are expected to solve. NEVER go into an oral without knowledge of the duties and responsibilities of the job you seek.

### 3) Think through each qualification required

Try to visualize the kind of questions you would ask if you were a board member. How well could you answer them? Try especially to appraise your own knowledge and background in each area, *measured against the job sought*, and identify any areas in which you are weak. Be critical and realistic – do not flatter yourself.

### 4) Do some general reading in areas in which you feel you may be weak

For example, if the job involves supervision and your past experience has NOT, some general reading in supervisory methods and practices, particularly in the field of human relations, might be useful. Do NOT study agency procedures or detailed manuals. The oral board will be testing your understanding and capacity, not your memory.

### 5) Get a good night's sleep and watch your general health and mental attitude

You will want a clear head at the interview. Take care of a cold or any other minor ailment, and of course, no hangovers.

*What should be done on the day of the interview?*

Now comes the day of the interview itself. Give yourself plenty of time to get there. Plan to arrive somewhat ahead of the scheduled time, particularly if your appointment is in the fore part of the day. If a previous candidate fails to appear, the board might be ready for you a bit early. By early afternoon an oral board is almost invariably behind schedule if there are many candidates, and you may have to wait. Take along a book or magazine to read, or your application to review, but leave any extraneous material in the waiting room when you go in for your interview. In any event, relax and compose yourself.

The matter of dress is important. The board is forming impressions about you – from your experience, your manners, your attitude, and your appearance. Give your personal appearance careful attention. Dress your best, but not your flashiest. Choose conservative, appropriate clothing, and be sure it is immaculate. This is a business interview, and your appearance should indicate that you regard it as such. Besides, being well groomed and properly dressed will help boost your confidence.

Sooner or later, someone will call your name and escort you into the interview room. *This is it.* From here on you are on your own. It is too late for any more preparation. But remember, you asked for this opportunity to prove your fitness, and you are here because your request was granted.

*What happens when you go in?*

The usual sequence of events will be as follows: The clerk (who is often the board stenographer) will introduce you to the chairman of the oral board, who will introduce you to the other members of the board. Acknowledge the introductions before you sit down. Do not be surprised if you find a microphone facing you or a stenotypist sitting by. Oral interviews are usually recorded in the event of an appeal or other review.

Usually the chairman of the board will open the interview by reviewing the highlights of your education and work experience from your application – primarily for the benefit of the other members of the board, as well as to get the material into the record. Do not interrupt or comment unless there is an error or significant misinterpretation; if that is the case, do not hesitate. But do not quibble about insignificant matters. Also, he will usually ask you some question about your education, experience or your present job – partly to get you to start talking and to establish the interviewing "rapport." He may start the actual questioning, or turn it over to one of the other members. Frequently, each member undertakes the questioning on a particular area, one in which he is perhaps most competent, so you can expect each member to participate in the examination. Because time is limited, you may also expect some rather abrupt switches in the direction the questioning takes, so do not be upset by it. Normally, a board member will not pursue a single line of questioning unless he discovers a particular strength or weakness.

After each member has participated, the chairman will usually ask whether any member has any further questions, then will ask you if you have anything you wish to add. Unless you are expecting this question, it may floor you. Worse, it may start you off on an extended, extemporaneous speech. The board is not usually seeking more information. The question is principally to offer you a last opportunity to present further qualifications or to indicate that you have nothing to add. So, if you feel that a significant qualification or characteristic has been overlooked, it is proper to point it out in a sentence or so. Do not compliment the board on the thoroughness of their examination – they have been sketchy, and you know it. If you wish, merely say, "No thank you, I have nothing further to add." This is a point where you can "talk yourself out" of a good impression or fail to present an important bit of information. Remember, *you close the interview yourself*.

The chairman will then say, "That is all, Mr. _____, thank you." Do not be startled; the interview is over, and quicker than you think. Thank him, gather your belongings and take your leave. Save your sigh of relief for the other side of the door.

*How to put your best foot forward*

Throughout this entire process, you may feel that the board individually and collectively is trying to pierce your defenses, seek out your hidden weaknesses and embarrass and confuse you. Actually, this is not true. They are obliged to make an appraisal of your qualifications for the job you are seeking, and they want to see you in your best light. Remember, they must interview all candidates and a non-cooperative candidate may become a failure in spite of their best efforts to bring out his qualifications. Here are 15 suggestions that will help you:

**1) Be natural – Keep your attitude confident, not cocky**

If you are not confident that you can do the job, do not expect the board to be. Do not apologize for your weaknesses, try to bring out your strong points. The board is interested in a positive, not negative, presentation. Cockiness will antagonize any board member and make him wonder if you are covering up a weakness by a false show of strength.

**2) Get comfortable, but don't lounge or sprawl**

Sit erectly but not stiffly. A careless posture may lead the board to conclude that you are careless in other things, or at least that you are not impressed by the importance of the occasion. Either conclusion is natural, even if incorrect. Do not fuss with your clothing, a pencil or an ashtray. Your hands may occasionally be useful to emphasize a point; do not let them become a point of distraction.

**3) Do not wisecrack or make small talk**

This is a serious situation, and your attitude should show that you consider it as such. Further, the time of the board is limited – they do not want to waste it, and neither should you.

### 4) Do not exaggerate your experience or abilities

In the first place, from information in the application or other interviews and sources, the board may know more about you than you think. Secondly, you probably will not get away with it. An experienced board is rather adept at spotting such a situation, so do not take the chance.

### 5) If you know a board member, do not make a point of it, yet do not hide it

Certainly you are not fooling him, and probably not the other members of the board. Do not try to take advantage of your acquaintanceship – it will probably do you little good.

### 6) Do not dominate the interview

Let the board do that. They will give you the clues – do not assume that you have to do all the talking. Realize that the board has a number of questions to ask you, and do not try to take up all the interview time by showing off your extensive knowledge of the answer to the first one.

### 7) Be attentive

You only have 20 minutes or so, and you should keep your attention at its sharpest throughout. When a member is addressing a problem or question to you, give him your undivided attention. Address your reply principally to him, but do not exclude the other board members.

### 8) Do not interrupt

A board member may be stating a problem for you to analyze. He will ask you a question when the time comes. Let him state the problem, and wait for the question.

### 9) Make sure you understand the question

Do not try to answer until you are sure what the question is. If it is not clear, restate it in your own words or ask the board member to clarify it for you. However, do not haggle about minor elements.

### 10) Reply promptly but not hastily

A common entry on oral board rating sheets is "candidate responded readily," or "candidate hesitated in replies." Respond as promptly and quickly as you can, but do not jump to a hasty, ill-considered answer.

### 11) Do not be peremptory in your answers

A brief answer is proper – but do not fire your answer back. That is a losing game from your point of view. The board member can probably ask questions much faster than you can answer them.

### 12) Do not try to create the answer you think the board member wants

He is interested in what kind of mind you have and how it works – not in playing games. Furthermore, he can usually spot this practice and will actually grade you down on it.

### 13) Do not switch sides in your reply merely to agree with a board member

Frequently, a member will take a contrary position merely to draw you out and to see if you are willing and able to defend your point of view. Do not start a debate, yet do not surrender a good position. If a position is worth taking, it is worth defending.

**14) Do not be afraid to admit an error in judgment if you are shown to be wrong**

The board knows that you are forced to reply without any opportunity for careful consideration. Your answer may be demonstrably wrong. If so, admit it and get on with the interview.

**15) Do not dwell at length on your present job**

The opening question may relate to your present assignment. Answer the question but do not go into an extended discussion. You are being examined for a *new* job, not your present one. As a matter of fact, try to phrase ALL your answers in terms of the job for which you are being examined.

*Basis of Rating*

Probably you will forget most of these "do's" and "don'ts" when you walk into the oral interview room. Even remembering them all will not ensure you a passing grade. Perhaps you did not have the qualifications in the first place. But remembering them will help you to put your best foot forward, without treading on the toes of the board members.

Rumor and popular opinion to the contrary notwithstanding, an oral board wants you to make the best appearance possible. They know you are under pressure – but they also want to see how you respond to it as a guide to what your reaction would be under the pressures of the job you seek. They will be influenced by the degree of poise you display, the personal traits you show and the manner in which you respond.

ABOUT THIS BOOK

This book contains tests divided into Examination Sections. Go through each test, answering every question in the margin. We have also attached a sample answer sheet at the back of the book that can be removed and used. At the end of each test look at the answer key and check your answers. On the ones you got wrong, look at the right answer choice and learn. Do not fill in the answers first. Do not memorize the questions and answers, but understand the answer and principles involved. On your test, the questions will likely be different from the samples. Questions are changed and new ones added. If you understand these past questions you should have success with any changes that arise. Tests may consist of several types of questions. We have additional books on each subject should more study be advisable or necessary for you. Finally, the more you study, the better prepared you will be. This book is intended to be the last thing you study before you walk into the examination room. Prior study of relevant texts is also recommended. NLC publishes some of these in our Fundamental Series. Knowledge and good sense are important factors in passing your exam. Good luck also helps. So now study this Passbook, absorb the material contained within and take that knowledge into the examination. Then do your best to pass that exam.

# EXAMINATION SECTION

# EXAMINATION SECTION
# TEST 1

DIRECTIONS: Each question or incomplete statement is followed by several suggested answers or completions. Select the one that BEST answers the question or completes the statement. *PRINT THE LETTER OF THE CORRECT ANSWER IN THE SPACE AT THE RIGHT.*

NOTE: The title of Agent refers to Sanitation Enforcement Agent, the office title of Sergeant refers to Level I of Associate Sanitation Enforcement Agent, and the office title of Lieutenant refers to Level II of Associate Sanitation Enforcement Agent.

The terms *N.O.V.* and *summons* are used interchangeably to refer to a Notice of Violation; *B.C.C.* refers to the Bureau of Cleaning and Collection; *see* refers to an in-field meeting between a Sanitation Enforcement Agent and a supervisor; and *R.T.* refers to the Assault Response Team.

Questions 1-2.

DIRECTIONS: Questions 1 and 2 are to be answered on the basis of the following fact pattern.

While Agent Wells was issuing an N.O.V. in front of a store at 110 Washington Boulevard, a man ran by, grabbed the Agent's uniform hat, and ran around the corner into an apartment building at 159 Jefferson Street. Agent Wells then contacts Sergeant Murray, who reports to the location to investigate. Later that day, in the zone office, Sergeant Murray is filling out a Report of Lost and Stolen Equipment form.

1. What should Sergeant Murray enter on the Report of Lost and Stolen Equipment form to identify the location where the uniform hat was lost or stolen?

   A. 159 Washington Boulevard
   B. 159 Jefferson Street
   C. 110 Washington Boulevard
   D. 110 Jefferson Street

2. What should Sergeant Murray enter on the Report of Lost and Stolen Equipment form to describe how the uniform hat was lost or stolen?

   A. Hat lost in store.
   B. Hat grabbed off head.
   C. Hat blown away by wind.
   D. Hat stolen out of car.

Questions 3-5.

DIRECTIONS: Questions 3 through 5 are to be answered on the basis of Command Order No. 86-57AE (Enforcement Procedures -Local Law 30 regarding posting) and the fact pattern below.

While on routine patrol, Sergeant Simpson observes three men outside an unoccupied private construction site that is surrounded by a plywood fence. Two of the men are hanging posters advertising a Two Brothers concert that is being arranged by King of Music Promotions, Inc. One of these men is pasting the posters onto the fence, while the other is affixing posters to lampposts in front of the construction site. The third man is ripping down old posters from the fence and throwing them on the sidewalk. When Sergeant Simpson questions the three men, he is told that nobody from King of Music Promotions, Inc. has contacted the City Council, Board of Estimate, Bureau of Franchises, or any other city agent about the posters.

3. Which of the following actions should Sergeant Simpson take regarding the man ripping down the old posters?

   A. Personally serve the man ripping down the posters with a summons for littering.
   B. Serve the construction site with a summons for Dirty Sidewalk using alternative service.
   C. Personally serve the man ripping down the posters with a summons for Unlawful Removal of posters.
   D. Allow the man to proceed since there is no violation.

4. Which of the following actions should Sergeant Simpson take regarding the man affixing the posters to the lampposts?

   A. Personally serve the man affixing posters to the lampposts with a summons for illegal posting.
   B. Serve the President of King of Music Promotions, Inc. with a summons for illegal posting using alternative service.
   C. Refer the violation to the Enforcement Division Posting Unit.
   D. Allow the man to proceed since there is no violation.

5. Which of the following actions should Sergeant Simpson take regarding the man pasting posters onto the plywood fence?

   A. Personally serve the man pasting the posters on the fence with a summons for illegal posting.
   B. Serve the President of King of Music Promotions, Inc. with a summons for illegal posting using alternative service.
   C. Refer the violation to the Enforcement Division Posting Unit.
   D. Allow the man to proceed since there is no violation.

6. While Sergeant Saunders is investigating a complaint against Ward TV and Appliances, the manager attempts to hand a folded twenty dollar bill to Sergeant Saunders and asks him if this will take care of the problem.
   In accordance with Mayor's Executive Order 16, Sergeant Saunders should

   A. report the incident directly and without undue delay to the Commissioner or an Inspector General
   B. tell the store manager that he will receive a summons for attempted bribery the next time he offers money
   C. take the money to headquarters, submit it as evidence of the incident, and document his actions on his Daily Activity Report
   D. call the Zone Lieutenant to notify him of the incident

7. There are many violations in a large public housing project located in one of Sergeant Washington's districts. Therefore, in accordance with Command Order 87-30E (regarding issuance to publicly owned property), Sergeant Washington should direct the assigned Agent to issue one summons

7._____

   A. each day until the violations are corrected
   B. each thirty-day period starting from the date of last issuance until the violations are corrected
   C. each fifteen-day period starting from the date of last issuance until the violations are corrected
   D. for each violation observed each day until the violations are corrected

Questions 8-11.

DIRECTIONS: Questions 8 through 11 are to be answered on the basis of the fact pattern below and the Worker's Compensation Board Form shown on the following page.

On July 6, 2006, Sergeant Parker is transporting Agent Donald Smith to Central County Hospital after an incident of assault against the Agent. The hospital is located at 1864 Shore Parkway, Bronx, N.Y. 10464. At the hospital, the attending physician, Dr. Larry Major, advises Agent Smith to remain overnight for observation. Agent Smith consents. Sergeant Parker then contacts headquarters to notify Agent Smith's nearest relative, Lillian Smith of 298 New Jersey Ave., Bronx, N.Y. 10450.

Later that day, Sergeant Parker is filling out a Worker's Compensation form for Agent Smith.

## WORKERS' COMPENSATION BOARD

|  |  |  | DATE OF ACCIDENT |
|---|---|---|---|
| Employer | THE CITY OF NEW YORK | Department Address | |
| Self Insured | THE CITY OF NEW YORK | LAW DEPARTMENT | |
| INJURED PERSON | (First) (Middle) (Last Name) | (Home Address) | |

Civil Service Title of Injured Person

REMARKS: _____

Is injured still under care of a physician? _____ If so, give name of physician: _____
Has injured died? _____ If so, state date of death: _____
NAME and ADDRESS of nearest relative known: _____

DATE of this REPORT _____                         THE CITY OF NEW YORK

Employee's S.S. No. _____        Signature _____
                                  Official Title _____

8. Which one of the following should Sergeant Parker enter in the box headed *Civil Service Title of Injured Person*?

    A. Associate Sanitation Enforcement Agent
    B. Sanitation Enforcement Officer
    C. Sanitation Enforcement Agent
    D. Issuing Officer

9. Which one of the following should Sergeant Parker enter in the space *Name and Address of Nearest Relative Known*?

    A. Lillian Smith, 298 New Jersey Ave., Bronx, NY 10450
    B. Lillian Smith, 1864 Shore Parkway, Bronx, NY 10464
    C. Donald Smith, 298 New Jersey Ave., Bronx, NY 10450
    D. Donald Smith, 1864 Shore Parkway, Bronx, NY 10464

10. Which one of the following should be entered in the space *If so, give name of physician*?

    A. Dr. Garry Major          B. Dr. Larry Major
    C. Dr. Garry Mason          D. Dr. Larry Mason

11. Which one of the following should Sergeant Parker enter in the box headed *Date of Accident*?  11._____

    A. June 6, 2006
    B. June 7, 2006
    C. July 6, 2006
    D. July 7, 2006

12. Sergeant Bill Bradford is checking Agent Cynthia Taylor's summons book at an announced *see* location. He observes that Agent Taylor has issued two summonses for K09 violations that she observed while on her way to her assigned district.  12._____
    Sergeant Bradford should

    A. sign Agent Taylor's Daily Summons Summary Report since the summonses were issued appropriately
    B. issue an Official Letter of Warning to Agent Taylor for issuing summonses out of district
    C. void the summonses since they were issued by an Agent who was out of her assigned district
    D. order an Agent who is assigned to the district in which the violations occurred to reissue the summonses

13. At 11:45 A.M., Sergeant Paula Adams radios to Agent John McCoy to schedule a *see* at 1:30 P.M. At 1:25 P.M., Sergeant Adams arrives at the location of the scheduled *see* at Wood Street in Section 21. Sergeant Adams cannot located Agent McCoy anywhere in the immediate area. Sgt. Adams should  13._____

    A. start searching Section 21 for Agent McCoy
    B. call headquarters for further instructions
    C. call Agent McCoy on the radio to ask for his estimated time of arrival
    D. wait five minutes and, if Agent McCoy does not appear, resume patrol and question him later concerning his whereabouts

14. While on the way to a scheduled *see* location, Sergeant Clark observes a citizen who fails to remove his dog's waste from the sidewalk.  14._____
    Sergeant Clark should

    A. obtain identification from the citizen and issue an N.O.V., then continue to the *see* location
    B. radio the Agent assigned to that section to come to the location to issue an N.O.V., then detain the citizen until the Agent arrives
    C. obtain identification from the citizen and issue an N.O.V., then stake-out the area for additional canine violations
    D. radio the Agent assigned to that section to come to the location immediately to issue an N.O.V. before the citizen leaves the area, then continue to the *see* location

Question 15.

DIRECTIONS: Question 15 is to be answered on the basis of the Notice of Violation and the Request to Void Summons Form and the fact pattern shown below and on the following page.

Agent Brown observes a Dirty Sidewalk violation at 1394 Gotham Boulevard, Long Island Railroad property. His attempts to locate a responsible party are to no avail. As Agent Brown is alternatively serving the summons at the location, Sergeant Harwood arrives for a *see*. Sergeant Harwood looks at the summons and tells Agent Brown that it must be voided. Sergeant Harwood directs Agent Brown to fill in the top part of a Request to Void Summons Form.

REQUEST TO VOID SUMMONS FORM
CITY OF NEW YORK DEPARTMENT OF SANITATION

TO: (ADJUDICATING AGENCY - ECB - PVB)
FROM: SUMMONS CONTROL UNIT
SUBJECT: REQUEST TO VOID SUMMONS

DATE  7/18/06

SUMMONS #  E051245691

ISSUING OFFICER/AGENT
(print name)  Jack Brown

VIOLATION  506

REGISTRY #  408813

ISSUING DATE  7/18/06

COMMAND  Brooklyn West 12

TIME SERVED  1:30 P.M.

BOROUGH  Brooklyn

PLACE OF OCCURRENCE  1394 Gotham Boulevard

REMARKS

ISSUING OFFICER/AGENT SIGNATURE

APPROVED BY
(Supv. Signature)
SUPV. TITLE

**No. E05 1 245 691** — ENVIRONMENTAL CONTROL BOARD NOTICE OF VIOLATION AND HEARING FOR CIVIL PENALTIES ONLY

City of New York, Petitioner vs Respondent:

- LAST NAME (Print): Long Island Railroad
- STREET ADDRESS: 1394 Gotham Blvd.
- CITY: Brooklyn  STATE: NY  ZIP: 11212

Date of Offense: 7/18/06  Time: 1:30 PM  County: MX  B.O. No.: 12  Violation Code: S1016

Administrative Code: 5. Sanitation Provisions

SECTION: 16-118(2)

At: Front of  Place of Occurrence: 1394 Gotham Blvd.

DETAILS OF VIOLATION: Dirty sidewalk — I did observe pieces of glass, paper, cans, banana peels scattered on sidewalk.

ALTERNATIVE SERVICE — Commercial

Maximum Penalty For Violation: $250.00

Date of Appearance: 10th Day of Aug 2006  1 X  8:30 AM

RANK (TITLE) SIGNATURE OF COMPLAINANT: SEA Jack Brown
REPORT LEVEL: E K 1 2
COMPLAINANT'S NAME (Printed): Jack Brown
TAX REGISTRY NUMBER: 4018113  AGENCY: 827
IS AFFIDAVIT OF SERVICE ON REVERSE SIDE SIGNED? ☒ YES  Date: 7/18/06

---

15. In order to complete the Request to Void Summons Form (DS 154), Sergeant Harwood must make an entry in the *Remarks* section and sign the form.
Which of the following should Sergeant Harwood enter in the *Remarks* section? No reissue -

    A. the Department only issues to Long Island Railroad property once every thirty days
    B. the Department only issues to Long Island Railroad property once every sixty days

C. only B.C.C. Supervisors are authorized to issue N.O.V.'s to Long Island Railroad property
D. Long Island Railroad is exempt from Sanitation Enforcement action

16. While Sergeant Lake is at the scene of an accident involving an injury to an Agent, he receives a radio transmission from Agent Marilyn Grant. Agent Grant informs him that she is attempting to issue a summons to a grocery store, but the owner refuses to give proper I.D. Agent Grant requests assistance.
Sergeant Lake informs the Agent that he is unable to assist her and should direct Agent Grant to

   A. resume patrol
   B. issue a nail-and-mail N.O.V.
   C. request assistance from another Agent
   D. radio headquarters to request assistance from a police sector car

16.___

17. During his 2:30 P.M. *see* with trainee Agent Grace Chan, Sergeant George Barry finds out that earlier in the afternoon she had written a nail-and-mail summons for three uncovered receptacles to a single-family dwelling.
In accordance with Department Violation Issuance Policies, Sergeant Barry should

   A. direct Agent Chan to issue summonses to other residences on the street
   B. advise Agent Chan that in this situation she can issue nail-and-mail summonses only if directed to do so by a District Superintendent or Enforcement Superior
   C. suggest that Agent Chan return to the street where the summons was issued and issue warning notices to the other residents on the street
   D. tell Agent Chan that she should have notified the District Superintendent or an Enforcement Supervisor directly after issuing the summons

17.___

18. Sergeant Glass is reviewing a summons that Agent Scott has just written to Teddy's Book Store for an *A* frame violation. Agent Scott explains that the summons was written in response to a letter of complaint from the Community Board, which states *check location for A frame and take corrective action*. Sergeant Glass then observes that the *A* frame is placed on a twelve foot wide sidewalk at the curb.
Sergeant Glass should inform Agent Scott that his action in writing the summons is

   A. *incorrect;* chiefly because the *A* frame was not a food-related *A* frame
   B. *correct;* chiefly because the community board asked the Department to take corrective action
   C. *incorrect;* chiefly because a warning should have been issued first
   D. *correct;* chiefly because the *A* frame should have been placed next to the building

18.___

19. When issuing personal service summonses, which of the following is ACCEPTABLE as primary proper identification?

   A. Social Security Card
   B. Voter Registration Card
   C. Current Motor Vehicle Registration
   D. Current New York City Pistol Permit

19.___

20. When issuing personal service summonses, which of the following is ACCEPTABLE as secondary proper identification?  20._____

    A. Utility bill
    B. Foreign passport
    C. New York State Notary Public Identification Card
    D. Business card with name, address, and telephone number

## KEY (CORRECT ANSWERS)

| | | | |
|---|---|---|---|
| 1. | C | 11. | C |
| 2. | B | 12. | A |
| 3. | A | 13. | C |
| 4. | A | 14. | A |
| 5. | D | 15. | D |
| 6. | A | 16. | B |
| 7. | B | 17. | B |
| 8. | C | 18. | C |
| 9. | A | 19. | D |
| 10. | B | 20. | C |

# EXAMINATION SECTION
# TEST 1

DIRECTIONS: Each question or incomplete statement is followed by several suggested answers or completions. Select the one that *BEST* answers the question or completes the statement. *PRINT THE LETTER OF THE CORRECT ANSWER IN THE SPACE AT THE RIGHT.*

Questions 1-5.

DIRECTIONS: Questions 1 through 5, inclusive, consist of groups of four displays representing license identification plates. Examine each group of plates and determine the number of plates in each group which are identical. Mark your answer sheets as follows:

If only two plates are identical, mark answer A.
If only three plates are identical, mark answer B.
If all four plates are identical, mark answer C.
If the plates are all different, mark answer D.

*EXAMPLE*

| ABC123 | BCD123 | ABC123 | BCD235 |

Since only two plates are identical, the first and the third, the correct answer is A.

1. PBV839    PVB839    PVB839    PVB839      1.___

2. WTX083    WTX083    WTX083    WTX083      2.___

3. B73609    D73906    BD7396    BD7906      3.___

4. AK7423    AK7423    AK1423    A81324      4.___

5. 583Y10    683Y10    583Y01    583Y10      5.___

Questions 6-10.

DIRECTIONS: Questions 6 through 10 consist of groups of numbers and letters similar to those which might appear on license plates. Each group of numbers and letters will be called a license identification. Choose the license identification lettered A, B, C, or D that *EXACTLY* matches the license identifcation shown next to the question number.

11

2 (#1)

*SAMPLE*

NY 1977
ABC - 123

A. NY 1976 ABC - 123
B. NY 1977 ABC - 132
C. NY 1977 CBA - 123
D. NY 1977 ABC - 123

The license identification given is NY 1977 ABC-123. The only choice that exactly matches it is the license identification next to the letter D. The correct answer is therefore D.

6. NY 1976 QLT 781

   A. NJ 1976 QLT 781
   B. NY 1975 QLT 781
   C. NY 1976 QLT 781
   D. NY 1977 QLT 781

7. FLA 1977 2-7LT58J

   A. FLA 1977 2-7TL58J
   B. FLA 1977 2-7LTJ58
   C. FLA 1977 2-7LT58J
   D. LA 1977 2-7LT58J

8. NY 1975 OQC383

   A. NY 1975 OQC383
   B. NY 1975 OQC883
   C. NY 1975 OCQ383
   D. NY 1977 OCQ383

9. MASS 1977 B-8DK02

   A. MISS 1977 B-8DK02
   B. MASS 1977 B-8DK02
   C. MASS 1976 B-8DK02
   D. MASS 1977 B-80KD2

10. NY 1976 ZV0586

    A. NY 1976 2V0586
    B. NY 1977 ZV0586
    C. NY 1976 ZV0586
    D. NY 1976 ZU0586

6.____
7.____
8.____
9.____
10.____

Questions 11-15.

DIRECTIONS: In copying the addresses below from Column A to the same line in Column B, an Agent-in-Training made some errors. For each question numbered 11 to 15, if you find that the Agent made an error in
only *one* line, mark your answer A
only *two* lines, mark your answer B
only *three* lines, mark your answer C
all *four* lines, mark your answer D

*EXAMPLE*

| Column A | Column B |
| --- | --- |
| 24 Third Avenue | 24 Third Avenue |
| 5 Lincoln Road | 5 Lincoln Street |
| 50 Central Park West | 6 Central Park West |
| 37-21 Queens Boulevard | 21-37 Queens Boulevard |

Since errors were made on only three lines, namely the second, third, and fourth, the correct answer is C.

| | Column A | Column B | |
| --- | --- | --- | --- |
| 11. | 57-22 Springfield Boulevard<br>94 Gun Hill Road<br>8 New Dorp Lane<br>36 Bedford Avenue | 75-22 Springfield Boulevard<br>94 Gun Hill Avenue<br>8 New Drop Lane<br>36 Bedford Avenue | 11.____ |
| 12. | 538 Castle Hill Avenue<br>54-15 Beach Channel Drive<br>21 Ralph Avenue<br>162 Madison Avenue | 538 Castle Hill Avenue<br>54-15 Beach Channel Drive<br>21 Ralph Avenue<br>162 Morrison Avenue | 12.____ |
| 13. | 49 Thomas Street<br>27-21 Northern Blvd.<br>86 125th Street<br>872 Atlantic Ave. | 49 Thomas Street<br>21-27 Northern Blvd.<br>86 125th Street<br>872 Baltic Ave. | 13.____ |
| 14. | 261-17 Horace Harding Expressway<br>191 Fordham Road<br>6 Victory Blvd.<br>552 Oceanic Ave. | 261-17 Horace Harding Parkway<br>191 Fordham Road<br>6 Victoria Blvd.<br>552 Ocean Ave. | 14.____ |
| 15. | 90-05 38th Avenue<br>19 Central Park West<br>9281 Avenue X<br>22 West Farms Square | 90-05 36th Avenue<br>19 Central Park East<br>9281 Avenue X<br>22 West Farms Square | 15.____ |

16. A parking enforcement agent must become a special patrolman in order to issue summonses. A summons is a written legal order, in the name of The People of the State, signed by a special patrolman, which requires the person to whom addressed to appear and answer the patrolman's charge at a specified time, date, and place.
According to the paragraph above, the reason that a parking enforcement agent is required to become a special patrolman is that a special patrolman is authorized to

    A. carry a loaded weapon
    B. answer specified charges from The People of the State
    C. serve a summons in the city
    D. adopt new parking regulations for the city

17. All summonses and stubs which have been issued to a parking enforcement agent must be accounted for by that agent. The agent must report to the district commander, without delay, any such summons or copy that has been damaged, lost, or stolen, or contains errors. Members of the force are not permitted to make changes or corrections on a summons or copy.
According to the paragraph above, the rule about correcting errors on a summons is that the

    A. district commander makes all changes on the summons
    B. parking enforcement agent makes changes on a copy of the summons
    C. parking enforcement agent makes changes on a damaged copy of the summons only
    D. summons must not be changed in any way

18. A procedure of the traffic control bureau concerned with the issuance of a summons for overtime parking in a metered space states:
    A summons shall be served by placing it under the windshield wiper.
Which one of the following possible reasons for this procedure is the MOST logical?

    A. Passing motorists will be made aware of the parking restrictions.
    B. The driver will see it and then put a coin into the meter.
    C. A passing police officer will see it and issue another summons.
    D. The summons is less likely to be lost before the driver returns.

19. If you find that there are not enough blank lines on a standard departmental report form to include all of the information you want to write in, how should you complete your report?

    A. Put this form aside and write your report on a blank paper
    B. Leave out some details called for on the report which seem unimportant
    C. Double the number of written lines by reducing your lettering to half-size
    D. Attach another sheet with the additional information written on it

20. Summonses must be served in numerical order. Which one of the following sequences of nine-digit numbers is in the correct numerical order?

    A. 69 088175-9; 69 088175-8; 69 088175-5; 69 088175-6
    B. 69 316958-4; 69 316958-5; 69 316958-6; 69 316958-7
    C. 68 088176-1; 68 088176-3; 68 088176-5; 68 088176-2
    D. 68 316950-5; 68 316950-2; 68 316950-3; 68 316950-4

# KEY (CORRECT ANSWERS)

1. B
2. C
3. D
4. A
5. A

6. C
7. C
8. A
9. B
10. C

11. C
12. A
13. B
14. C
15. B

16. C
17. D
18. D
19. D
20. B

# TEST 2

DIRECTIONS: Each question or incomplete statement is followed by several suggested answers or completions. Select the one that BEST answers the question or completes the statement. PRINT THE LETTER OF THE CORRECT ANSWER IN THE SPACE AT THE RIGHT.

Questions 1-20.

DIRECTIONS: Each of Questions 1 through 20 consists of a sentence in which a word is italicized. Of the four words following each sentence, choose the word whose meaning is most nearly the SAME as the meaning of the italicized word.

1. The Agent's first *assignment* was to patrol on Hicks Avenue.
   A. test   B. sign   C. job   D. deadline

2. Agents get many *inquiries* from the public.
   A. complaints   B. suggestions
   C. compliments   D. questions

3. The names of all fifty states were written in *abbreviated* form.
   A. shortened   B. corrected   C. eliminated   D. illegible

4. The meter was examined and found to be *defective*.
   A. small   B. operating   C. destroyed   D. faulty

5. Agent Roger's reports are *legible*, but Agent Baldwin's are not.
   A. similar   B. readable   C. incorrect   D. late

6. The time allowed, as shown by the meter, had *expired*.
   A. started   B. broken   C. ended   D. violated

7. The busy *commercial* area is quiet in the evenings.
   A. deserted   B. growing   C. business   D. local

8. The district office *authorized* the giving of summonses to illegally parked trucks.
   A. suggested   B. approved   C. prohibited   D. recorded

9. Department property must be used *exclusively* for official business.
   A. occasionally   B. frequently   C. only   D. properly

10. The District Commander *banned* driving in the area.
    A. detoured   B. permitted   C. encouraged   D. prohibited

11. Two copies of the summons are *retained* by the Parking Enforcement Agent.
    A. kept   B. distributed   C. submitted   D. signed

1.___
2.___
3.___
4.___
5.___
6.___
7.___
8.___
9.___
10.___
11.___

16

12. The Agent *detected* a parking violation.  12._____

    A. cancelled   B. discovered   C. investigated   D. reported

13. *Pedestrians* may be given summonses for violating traffic regulations.  13._____

    A. bicycle riders         B. horsemen
    C. motorcyclists          D. walkers

14. Parked cars are not allowed to *obstruct* traffic.  14._____

    A. direct   B. lead   C. block   D. speed

15. It was *obvious* to the Agent that the traffic light was broken.  15._____

    A. uncertain   B. surprising   C. possible   D. clear

16. The signs stated that parking in the area was *restricted* to vehicles of foreign diplomats.  16._____

    A. allowed   B. increased   C. desired   D. limited

17. Each parking violation carries an *appropriate* fine.  17._____

    A. suitable   B. extra   C. light   D. heavy

18. Strict enforcement of parking regulations helps to *alleviate* traffic congestion.  18._____

    A. extend   B. build   C. relieve   D. increase

19. The Traffic Control Bureau has a rule which states that an Agent shall speak and act *courteously* in any relationship with the public.  19._____

    A. respectfully       B. timidly
    C. strangely          D. intelligently

20. City traffic regulations prohibit parking at *jammed* meters.  20._____

    A. stuck   B. timed   C. open   D. installed

# KEY (CORRECT ANSWERS)

| | | | |
|---|---|---|---|
| 1. | C | 11. | A |
| 2. | D | 12. | B |
| 3. | A | 13. | D |
| 4. | D | 14. | C |
| 5. | B | 15. | D |
| 6. | C | 16. | D |
| 7. | C | 17. | A |
| 8. | B | 18. | C |
| 9. | C | 19. | A |
| 10. | D | 20. | A |

# EXAMINATION SECTION
# TEST 1

DIRECTIONS: Each question or incomplete statement is followed by several suggested answers or completions. Select the one that *BEST* answers the question or completes the statement. *PRINT THE LETTER OF THE CORRECT ANSWER IN THE SPACE AT THE RIGHT.*

Questions 1-6.

DIRECTIONS: Questions 1 through 6 are based on the following reading passage covering PROCEDURES FOR PATROL. When answering these questions, refer to this passage.

## PROCEDURES FOR PATROL

The primary function of all Parking Enforcement Agents assigned to patrol duty shall be to patrol assigned areas and issue summonses to violators of various sections of the City Traffic Regulations, which sections govern the parking or operation of vehicles. Parking Enforcement Agents occasionally may be called upon to distribute educational pamphlets and perform other work, at the discretion of the Bureau Chief.

Each Agent on patrol duty will be assigned a certain area (or areas) to be patrolled each day. These areas will be assigned during the daily roll call. Walking Cards will describe the street locations of the patrol and the manner in which the patrol is to be walked.

A Traffic Department vehicle will be provided for daily patrol assignments when necessary. Each Agent shall accomplish an assigned field patrol in the following manner:
  a. Start each patrol at the location specified on the daily patrol sheet, and proceed as per walking instructions.
  b. Approach each metered space being utilized (each metered space in which a vehicle is parked). If the meter shows the expired flag, the member of the force shall prepare and affix a summons to the vehicle parked at meter.
  c. Any vehicle in violation of any regulation governing the parking, standing, stopping, or movement of vehicles will be issued a summons.
  d. No summons will be issued to a vehicle displaying an authorized vehicle identification plate of the Police Department unless the vehicle is parked in violation of the No Standing, No Stopping, Hydrant, Bus Stop, or Double Parking Regulations. Identification plates for Police Department automobiles are made of plastic and are of rectangular shape, 10 3/4" long, 3 3/4" high, black letters and numerals on a white background. The words "POLICE DEPT." are printed on the face with the identification number. In addition, the Police Department emblem is printed on each card. Identification plates for private automobiles are the same size and shape as those used on Police Department automobiles.

An Agent on patrol, when observing a person "feeding" a street meter (placing an additional coin in a meter so as to leave the vehicle parked for an additional period) shall prepare and affix a summons to the vehicle.

An Agent on patrol shall note on a computer card each missing or defective, out of order, or otherwise damaged meter.

1. Of the following, the work which the Parking Enforcement Agent performs MOST often is

    A. issuing summonses for parking violations
    B. distributing educational pamphlets
    C. assisting the Bureau Chief
    D. driving a City vehicle

2. The area to be covered by a Parking Enforcemeng Agent on patrol is

    A. determined by the Police Department
    B. regulated by the City Traffic Regulations
    C. marked off with red flags
    D. described on Walking Cards

3. A Parking Enforcement Agent reports a broken meter by

    A. issuing a summons
    B. making a mark on a computer card
    C. raising the flag on the broken meter
    D. attending a daily roll call

4. With respect to the use of an automobile for patrol duty,

    A. Parking Enforcement Agents must supply their own cars for patrol
    B. automobiles for patrol will be supplied by the Police Department
    C. Parking Enforcement Agents are permitted to park in a bus stop
    D. department vehicles will be provided when required for patrol

5. Parking Enforcement Agents sometimes issue summonses to drivers for "feeding" a street meter in violation of parking regulations. Which one of the following situations describes such a violation? A driver

    A. has moved from one metered space to another
    B. has parked next to a Police Department No Standing sign
    C. is parked by a meter which shows 30 minutes time still remaining
    D. has used a coin to reset the meter after his first time period expired

6. Vehicles displaying an authorized vehicle identification plate of the Police Department are allowed to park at expired meters. Which one of the following statements describes the proper size of identification plates for *private automobiles used for police work*? They

    A. are 10 3/4" long, and 3 3/4" high
    B. have white letters and numerals on a black background
    C. are 3 3/4" long, and 10 3/4" high
    D. have black letters and numerals on a white background

7. If a parking enforcement agent is questioned by an angry driver who has just been given a summons for violation of a parking regulation, which one of the following replies by the agent would be MOST likely to retain the good will of the complaining driver?

    A. "Let me explain as best I can the reasons for my action."
    B. "I'm only doing the job I'm getting paid for, so don't get mad at me."
    C. "I don't make the parking regulations, I just have to uphold them."
    D. "The City's rules and regulations are made to be obeyed by everyone."

8. One day, during the absence of her regular supervisor, a temporary supervisor assigns Jane Brown to a patrol car that she has worked before, but instructs her to carry out this assignment in a way which is different from her usual instructions.
   Which one of the following actions *BEST* fulfills Agent Brown's responsibility as a parking enforcement agent?

   A. Follow the instructions of her temporary supervisor without comment
   B. Explain to this supervisor how this work has been done in the past
   C. If she thinks that past instructions were better, Brown should disregard any new instructions
   D. Ask the other agents what they are going, and follow their lead

9. Parking enforcement agents should wear their badges only when in uniform or as ordered by the bureau chief. The badge must be displayed on the agent's outermost uniform garment on the area provided for the badge. An agent must immediately report the loss of a badge to the district commander, and must also submit a statement of the events leading up to the loss. The agent who lost the badge must pay for a new one.
   According to the paragraph above, one of the rules concerning the wearing of the badge by a parking enforcement agent is that

   A. the badge must be worn on the inside coat pocket at all times
   B. a temporary badge should be borrowed to replace a lost badge
   C. the badge must be worn where it can be seen on the uniform
   D. only bureau chiefs and district commanders are required to wear badges

10. As required by the traffic bureau's uniform specifications, parking enforcement agents must purchase their own uniforms. Uniforms appropriate for seasonal use must be displayed at semi-annual inspections. An annual uniform allowance is granted to all members of the force to cover the cost of their uniforms.
    According to the paragraph above, one of the rules concerning the purchase of uniforms is that

    A. the traffic bureau supplies uniforms to all parking enforcement agents
    B. parking enforcement agents are required to purchase their own uniforms
    C. parking enforcement agents only wear uniforms for semi-annual inspections
    D. parking enforcement agents select their own uniform colors

11. Inspection of uniforms is conducted in the parking enforcement agent's field office. Regular uniform inspection is held as follows:
        The winter uniform is inspected in May, and includes rain gear, jacket, overcoat, hat, skirt or trousers, shoes, boots (optional), ties (2), hood, shoulder bag, and gloves.
        The summer uniform, is inspected in January and includes rain gear, suit, cap, and gloves.
    According to the paragraph above, which one of the following lists contains the categories of uniform items which are included in *both* the winter and summer inspections?

    A. Shoes and gloves
    B. Suit, cap, and shoulder bag
    C. Rain gear, jacket, and overcoat
    D. Gloves and rain gear

12. When reporting for duty, a parking enforcement agent who is assigned to operate a department of traffic motor vehicle must carefully inspect the vehicle to see that it is in serviceable condition. When making the inspection, the operator must check to see that
    sufficient gasoline is in the tank and the proper amount of oil in the crankcase;
    the radiator is properly filled with water, and, when department orders require, sufficient anti-freeze is maintained in the radiator;
    brakes, lights, windshield wipers, and warning devices are working properly;
    tires, and spare, are properly inflated.
    According to the paragraph above, it is the responsibility of the operator of a department motor vehicle, before taking it on the road, to check the condition of the

    A. tires   B. engine   C. transmission   D. battery

13. A parking enforcement agent's immediate supervisor is the *BEST* source of information on the duties and responsibilities of the job. According to the procedures of the traffic control bureau:
    The chain of authority for the uniformed force shall be in the following order: Commissioner; bureau chief; assistant bureau chief; regional commander; district commander; squad leader; parking enforcement agent.
    Based on the procedure above, whom should a parking enforcement agent ask for help in filling out a daily report? The

    A. regional commander      B. squad leader
    C. bureau chief            D. district commander

14. According to the procedures of the traffic control bureau:
    A parking enforcement agent shall follow all lawful verbal and written instructions, policies, procedures, and any other directions of a superior officer; promptly inform a superior officer of any unusual occurrences; take no action involving physical force against any individual and, shall at all times, act in a manner which will further the aims of the city, the department, and the bureau.
    Based on the procedures above, what is the proper action to be taken by a parking enforcement agent upon observing what appears to be a robbery in progress?

    A. Watch everything that happens and make notes for a daily report
    B. Report the incident to a superior officer by the nearest telephone
    C. Assist the apparent victims to repel their attackers
    D. Continue on the assigned patrol, maintaining the normal schedule

Questions 15-20.

DIRECTIONS: Questions 15 through 20 are based on the following reading passage covering the OPERATION OF DEPARTMENT MOTOR VEHICLES. When answering these questions, refer to this passage.

OPERATION OF DEPARTMENT MOTOR VEHICLES

When operating a Traffic Department motor vehicle, a member of the force must show every courtesy to other drivers, obey all traffic signs and traffic regulations, obey all other lawful authority, and handle the vehicle in a manner which will foster safety practices in others and create a favorable impression of the Bureau, the Department, and the City. The operator and passengers must use the safety belts.

*Driving Rules* -
   a. *Do not* operate a mechanically defective vehicle.
      *Do not* race engine on starting.
      *Do not* tamper with mechanical equipment.
      *Do not* run engine if there is an indication of low engine oil pressure, overheating, or no transmission oil.
   b. When parking on highway, all safety precautions must be observed.
   c. When parking in a garage or parking field, observe a maximum speed of 5 miles per hour. Place shift lever in park or neutral position, effectively apply hand brake, then shut off all ignition and light switches to prevent excess battery drain, and close all windows.

*Reporting Defects* -
   a. Report all observed defects on Drivers' Vehicle Defect Card and on Monthly Vehicle Report Form 49 in sufficient detail so a mechanic can easily locate the source of trouble.
   b. Enter vehicle road service calls and actual time of occurrence on Monthly Vehicle Report.

*Reporting Accidents* -
Promptly report all facts of each accident as follows: For serious accidents, including those involving personal injury, call your supervisor as soon as possible. Give all the appropriate information about the accident to your supervisor.

Record vehicle registration information, including the name of the registered owner, the state, year, and serial number, and the classification marking on the license plates. Also record the operator's license number and other identifying information, and, if it applies, the injured person's age and sex.

Give a full description of how the accident happened, and what happened following the accident, including the vehicles in collision, witnesses, police badge number, hospital, condition of road surface, time of day, weather conditions, location (near, far, center of intersection), and damage.

*Repairs to Automobiles* -
When a Department motor vehicle requires repairs that cannot be made by the operator, or requires replacement of parts or accessories (including tires and tubes), or requires towing, the operator shall notify the District Commander.

When a Departmental motor vehicle is placed out of service for repairs, the Regional Commander shall assign another vehicle, if available.

*Daily Operator's Report* -
The operator of a Department automobile shall keep a daily maintenance record of the vehicle, and note any unusual occurrences, on the Daily Operator's Report.

15. Parking Enforcement Agents who are assigned to operate Department motor vehicles on patrol are expected to

   A. disregard the posted speed limits to save time
   B. remove their seat belts on short trips
   C. show courtesy to other drivers on the road
   D. take the right of way at all intersections

16. The driver of a Department motor vehicle should

   A. leave the windows open when parking the vehicle in a garage
   B. drive the vehicle at approximately 10 miles per hour in a parking field
   C. be alert for indication of low engine oil pressure and over-heated engine
   D. start a cold vehicle by racing the engine for 5 minutes

17. The reason that all defects on a Department vehicle that have been observed by its driver should be noted on a Monthly Vehicle Report Form 49 is:

   A. This action will foster better safety practices among other Agents
   B. The source of the defect may be located easily by a trained mechanic
   C. All the facts of an accident will be reported promptly
   D. The District Commander will not have to make road calls

18. If the driver of a Department vehicle is involved in an accident, an Accident Report should be made out. This Report should include a full description of how the accident happened.
   Which one of the following statements would PROPERLY belong in an Accident Report?

   A. "The accident occurred at the intersection of Broadway and 42nd Street."
   B. "The operator of the department vehicle replaced the windshield wiper."
   C. "The vehicle was checked for gas and water before the patrol began."
   D. "A bus passed two parked vehicles."

19. When a Department vehicle is disabled, whom should the operator notify? The

   A. Traffic Department garage        B. Assistant Bureau Chief
   C. Police Department                D. District Commander

20. The PROPER way for an operator of a Department vehicle to report unusual occurrences with respect to the operation of the vehicle is to

   A. follow the same procedures as for reporting a defect
   B. request the Regional Commander to assign another vehicle
   C. phone the Bureau Chief as soon as possible
   D. make a note of the circumstances on the Daily Operator's Report

## KEY (CORRECT ANSWERS)

| | | | |
|---|---|---|---|
| 1. | A | 11. | D |
| 2. | D | 12. | A |
| 3. | B | 13. | B |
| 4. | D | 14. | B |
| 5. | D | 15. | C |
| 6. | A | 16. | C |
| 7. | A | 17. | B |
| 8. | B | 18. | A |
| 9. | C | 19. | D |
| 10. | B | 20. | D |

# TEST 2

DIRECTIONS: Each question or incomplete statement is followed by several suggested answers or completions. Select the one that BEST answers the question or completes the statement. *PRINT THE LETTER OF THE CORRECT ANSWER IN THE SPACE AT THE RIGHT.*

Questions 1-5.

DIRECTIONS: Questions 1 through 5 are based on the following reading passage. When answering these questions, use *ONLY* the information in this passage.

Stopping, standing, and parking of motor vehicles is regulated by law to keep the public highways open for a smooth flow of traffic, and to keep stopped vehicles from blocking intersections, driveways, signs, fire hydrants, and other areas that must be kept clear. These established regulations apply in all situations, unless otherwise indicated by signs. Other local restrictions are posted in the areas to which they apply. Three examples of these other types of restrictions, which may apply singly or in combination with one another are:

NO STOPPING - This means that a driver may not stop a vehicle for any purpose except when necessary to avoid interference with other vehicles, or in compliance with directions of a police officer or signal.

NO STANDING - This means that a driver may stop a vehicle only temporarily to actually receive or discharge passengers.

NO PARKING - This means that a driver may stop a vehicle only temporarily to actually load or unload merchandise or passengers. When stopped, it is advisable to turn on warning flashers if equipped with them. However, one should never use a directional signal for this purpose, because it may confuse other drivers. Some NO PARKING signs prohibit parking between certain hours on certain days.

For example, the sign may read NO PARKING 8 A.M. to 11 A.M. MONDAY, WEDNESDAY, FRIDAY. These signs are usually utilized on streets where cleaning operations take place on alternate days

1. The parking regulation that applies to fire hydrants is an example of _____ regulations.   1.____

   A. local   B. established   C. posted   D. temporary

2. When stopped in a NO PARKING zone, it is *advisable* to   2.____

   A. turn on the right directional signal to indicate to other drivers that you will remain stopped
   B. turn on the left directional signal to indicate to other drivers that you may be leaving the curb after a period of time
   C. turn on the warning flashers if your car is equipped with them
   D. put the vehicle in reverse so that the backup lights will be on to warn approaching cars that you have temporarily stopped

3. You may stop a vehicle temporarily to discharge passengers in an area under the restriction of a   3.____

   A. NO STOPPING - NO STANDING zone
   B. NO STANDING - NO PARKING zone
   C. NO PARKING - NO STOPPING zone
   D. NO STOPPING - NO STANDING - NO PARKING zone

25

4. A sign reads "NO PARKING 8 A.M. to 11 A.M., MONDAY, WEDNESDAY, FRIDAY."  4.___
   Based on this sign, a parking enforcement agent would issue a summons to a car that is parked on a

   A. Tuesday at 9:30 a.m.    B. Wednesday at 12:00 a.m.
   C. Friday at 10:30 a.m.    D. Saturday at 8:00 a.m.

5. NO PARKING signs prohibiting parking between certain hours, on certain days, are usually utilized on streets where  5.___

   A. vehicles frequently take on and discharge passengers
   B. cleaning operations take place on alternate days
   C. NO STOPPING signs have been ignored
   D. commercial vehicles take on and unload merchandise

Questions 6-15.

DIRECTIONS: Questions 6 through 15 are based on the following reading passage. When answering these questions, use ONLY the information in this passage.

Parking Enforcement Agents in Iron City work three shifts. The first shift is from 10 a.m. to 6 p.m. The second shift is from 6 p.m. to 2 a.m. The third shift is from 2 a.m. to 10 a.m. Each shift at the Central Office employs three people who patrol the surrounding area. Parking Enforcement Agents have one hour off per shift for lunch.

Starting on Tuesday, Agents Fred Black, Mary Evans, and Thomas Hart worked the first shift. Harold Wilson and Mary Wood worked the second shift. The third agent for the second shift was ill. Thomas Hart worked the second shift in addition to his regular first shift, and thus earned overtime pay. Mike Brown, Anne Hill, and Jeff Smith worked the third shift.

On his first shift, Agent Thomas Hart wrote 11 summonses for meter violations, 15 summonses for double parking, and 13 summonses for parking in a no-standing zone. On his second shift, Thomas Hart wrote 21 summonses for double parking, 13 summonses for meter violations, and 15 summonses for parking in a no-standing zone.

6. On Tuesday, Agent Mary Wood was on duty from  6.___

   A. 6 a.m. to 2 p.m.    B. 10 a.m. to 6 p.m.
   C. 2 a.m. to 6 p.m.    D. 6 p.m. to 2 a.m.

7. How many Parking Enforcement Agents normally work from 6 p.m. to 2 a.m.?  7.___

   A. One    B. Two    C. Three    D. Four

8. The number of Parking Enforcement Agents who *actually* worked the second shift on Tuesday was  8.___

   A. one    B. two    C. three    D. four

9. Among the three successive shifts which started on Tuesday, the total number of DIFFERENT Parking Enforcement Agents who *actually* reported for duty was  9.___

   A. 7    B. 8    C. 9    D. 10

10. The total number of summonses Agent Hart wrote during the FIRST shift he worked was  10.___

    A. 11    B. 13    C. 39    D. 49

3 (#2)

11. Agent Hill was scheduled to finish her shift at

    A. 10 a.m.   B. 6 p.m.   C. 10 p.m.   D. 2 a.m.

12. Parking Enforcement Agents have one hour off per shift. The total hours *actually* worked by Agent Evans on Tuesday was

    A. 8 hours   B. 7 1/2 hours   C. 7 hours   D. 6 1/2 hours

13. The total number of summonses Agent Hart wrote for meter violations was

    A. 15   B. 24   C. 26   D. 34

14. During both his shifts, Agent Hart wrote the MOST summonses for

    A. A meter violations
    C. double parking
    B. standing in a no-parking zone
    D. parking in a no-standing zone

15. The total number of summonses Agent Hart wrote during his two shifts was

    A. 28   B. 48   C. 68   D. 88

Questions 16-20.

DIRECTIONS: Answer Questions 16 through 20 ONLY on the basis of the information contained in the street map and the accompanying explanatory information given below.

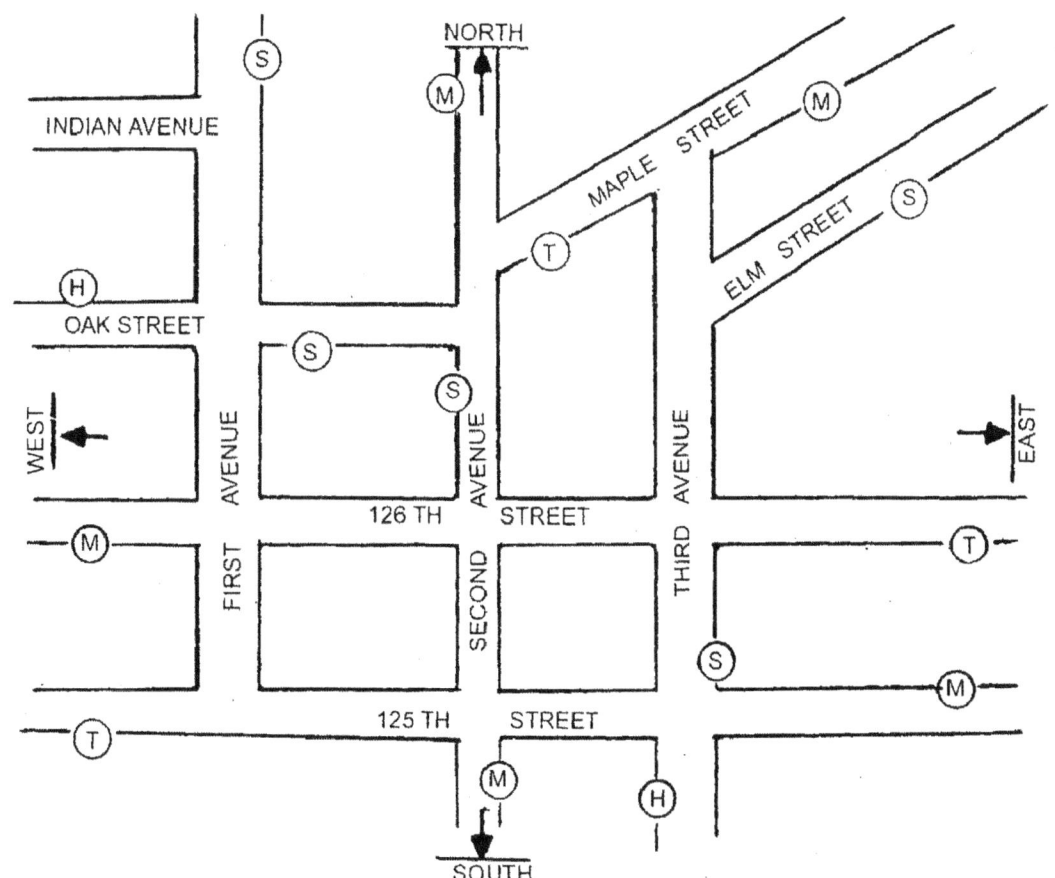

The map displayed above represents Parking Enforcement Agent Johnson's assigned area. The circled letters represent locations of special interest to him. Ⓜ is a meter location, Ⓗ is a fire hydrant location; Ⓢ is a bus stop; Ⓣ and is a taxi stand. Summonses are issued for parking at any of these locations.

16. Johnson was walking west on 126th Street. He made a left turn into 3rd Avenue. He issued a summons to a car parked on the east side of the street.
    For what type of violation did he issue this summons?

    A. Meter violation  
    C. Parked at a taxi stand  
    B. Parked at a fire hydrant  
    D. Parked at a bus stop

17. Johnson was walking south on 1st Avenue. He made a right turn into Oak Street. He issued a summons to a car parked on the north side of the street.
    For what type of violation did he issue this summons?

    A. Meter violation  
    C. Parked at a taxi stand  
    B. Parked at a fire hydrant  
    D. Parked at a bus stop

18. Johnson was walking east on 125th Street. He made a left turn into 3rd Avenue and, at the first intersection, turned right into another street. He then issued a summons to the car parked on the south side of the street.
    For what type of violation did he issue this summons?

    A. Meter violation  
    C. Parked at a taxi stand  
    B. Parked at a fire hydrant  
    D. Parked at a bus stop

19. Johnson was walking in a westerly direction on Maple Street. He made a left turn into 2nd Avenue and then made a left turn into 126th Street.
    In what direction would Jones be walking on 126th Street?

    A. East    B. North    C. West    D. South

20. As shown on the map, with only the locations indicated, how many DIFFERENT types of violations could Johnson issue summonses for on 2nd Avenue?

    A. 1    B. 2    C. 3    D. 4

## KEY (CORRECT ANSWERS)

| | | | |
|---|---|---|---|
| 1. | B | 11. | A |
| 2. | C | 12. | C |
| 3. | B | 13. | B |
| 4. | C | 14. | C |
| 5. | B | 15. | D |
| 6. | D | 16. | D |
| 7. | C | 17. | B |
| 8. | C | 18. | C |
| 9. | B | 19. | A |
| 10. | C | 20. | B |

# EXAMINATION SECTION
## TEST 1

DIRECTIONS: Each question or incomplete statement is followed by several suggested answers or completions. Select the one that BEST answers the question or completes the statement. *PRINT THE LETTER OF THE CORRECT ANSWER IN THE SPACE AT THE RIGHT.*

1. When a vehicle is so large that it must use two metered parking spaces, it should be parked

    A. with its front end alongside the forward meter and a coin deposited only in the forward meter
    B. with its front end alongside the forward meter and coins deposited in the meters for each, of the spaces filled by the vehicle
    C. with its tail end alongside the rear meter and a coin deposited in the meter closest to the rear of the vehicle
    D. in the approximate middle of the two spaces and a coin deposited in either of the meters alongside the vehicle

1.____

2. A senior enforcement agent finds the following cars parked at expired meters at a time when meter regulations are in effect:
    I. A vehicle with FC plates
    II. A vehicle with a Patrolman's Benevolent Association card on the sun visor
    III. An unmarked vehicle displaying a blue metal shield identifying it as a City Police Department car

    Which of the above vehicles should be given summonses?

    A. I, but not II and III
    C. I and II, but not III
    B. II, but not I and III
    D. II and III, but not I

2.____

3. An enforcement agent mistakenly issues a summons to an unoccupied automobile parked at a meter at a time when parking is not restricted. The agent realizes his error before the driver of the automobile returns.
In this situation, the agent should

    A. destroy the summons but make a note of the circumstnces under which it was issued on the back of the agency copy
    B. leave a note on the automobile to the motorist telling him to disregard the summons since it was issued in error
    C. allow the motorist to receive the summons since the error can be corrected later
    D. return the summons to the district commander with a written memo describing the circumstances under which it was issued

3.____

4. Following are three practices a senior enforcement agent observes while on patrol:
    I. A person reserving a parking space in front of a fruit store by placing a crate in the roadway
    II. A motorcycle five feet long parked at an angle to the curb with one wheel touching the curb
    III. A food vendor parked at a metered parking space selling sodas and ice cream to passing pedestrians

4.____

Which one of the following correctly classifies the above practices into those which are LAWFUL and those which are NOT?

- A. I is lawful, but II and III are not
- B. II is lawful, but I and III are not
- C. II and III are lawful, but I is not
- D. I, II and III are not lawful

5. The MAIN purpose of instructing department enforcement personnel to disregard fraternal, labor, social, religious, and political identifications on vehicles is to

- A. provide for impartial enforcement of regulations
- B. simplify the work of Parking Enforcement Agents
- C. make sure that no one group gets more summonses than any other group
- D. increase the number of summonses issued

6. During the absence of the district commander, one of the senior enforcement agents from that district may be assigned to perform the duties of the district commander. If no one has been specifically named to take over this job, the senior who takes over for the district commander is the one

- A. with the most seniority
- B. who reports to work first
- C. scheduled for a regular day off
- D. who has not previously substituted for the district commander

7. While you are checking an area, a motorist in a private car complains to you that an agent issued a summons to him for double parking but that a passenger car parked right behind him did not get a summons.
The BEST action for you to take is to tell him

- A. to give you all the information and you will investigate the matter
- B. to call the main office
- C. that it was probably just an oversight and you will speak to the agent
- D. that whether or not the other driver got a summons is not his business

8. Special Vehicle Identification permits issued to handicapped drivers permit the holders to park

- A. in areas regulated by "No Parking" signs
- B. in areas regulated by "No Stopping" signs
- C. at fire hydrants
- D. at taxi stands

9. The one of the following items which does NOT have to be entered on an enforcement agent's field patrol sheet is the

- A. report of an abandoned car which does not have a Sanitation Department sticker
- B. completion of Univac (computer) cards to report missing, defective or vandalized meters
- C. listing of the locations of the agent's personal and meal breaks
- D. notation that the agent observed collectors from a Finance Department truck collecting money from parking meters

10. Assume that standing is prohibited in a certain area. According to the traffic regulations, the driver of a passenger vehicle in that area would be permitted to

    A. stand in front of a private driveway
    B. stop to discharge passengers
    C. park temporarily in order to unload merchandise
    D. stand for a period of no more than ten minutes provided he remains in the car

11. According to the traffic regulations, the MINIMUM period of time a vehicle may be parked before it is considered to be parked for the principal purpose of storing the vehicle is

    A. 12 hours     B. 24 hours     C. 36 hours     D. 48 hours

12. An enforcement agent finds each of the following three vehicles parked on a street with no posted parking restrictions:
    I. A van with commercial plates which has been parked in front of a store for six hours
    II. A car parked at the curb while the owner is changing a flat tire
    III. A car parked in front of a private home while the owner is washing the car

    According to the traffic regulations, which one of the following CORRECTLY classifies the above vehicles into those which should receive summonses and those which should not?

    A. I and II should receive summonses, but III should not
    B. II and III should receive summonses, but I should not
    C. I and III should receive summonses, but II should not
    D. I, II, and III should receive summonses

13. A senior enforcement agent should inspect the uniform and equipment of each member of his squad at least once a

    A. day     B. week     C. pay-period     D. month

14. When a senior enforcement agent cannot locate the parking enforcement agent assigned to a patrol area, she notes this fact and the time on her field patrol sheet. According to bureau procedures the FIRST action the senior should take when she sees the missing agent is to

    A. order the agent to report to the district commander
    B. ask the agent for an explanation of the absence
    C. check the agent's field patrol sheet to see if there was a reason for the absence
    D. submit a report on the incident to the district commander

15. In addition to their daily enforcement duties, senior enforcement agents are generally required to

    A. accompany agents to a hospital when agents are injured or assaulted
    B. make out probationary reports on clerical personnel
    C. deliver completed summonses to the parking violations bureau
    D. deliver notices of special assignments to agents who are off duty

16. An enforcement agent should be instructed to issue a summons to a car    16.____

    A. that forms part of a funeral procession, double-parked in front of a funeral parlor
    B. with DPL plates parked in a "No Standing" zone
    C. with MD plates parked for two hours in front of a hospital
    D. that displays an SVI card parked in a "No Parking" zone

17. An enforcement agent observes the driver of a passenger vehicle discharging passen-    17.____
    gers at a bus stop.
    Of the following, the MOST appropriate action for the agent to take is to

    A. continue on patrol
    B. issue a summons
    C. warn the driver that what he is doing is illegal
    D. politely ask the driver to move

18. The *one* of the following who usually assigns enforcement agents to their daily patrol    18.____
    areas and rotates the agents from one patrol area to another is the

    A. senior enforcement agent
    B. district commander
    C. regional commander
    D. chief of the traffic control bureau

19. An enforcement agent on patrol discovers a traffic signal out of order.    19.____
    The FIRST of the following actions the agent should take is to

    A. regulate traffic at the intersection himself until repair service arrives
    B. inform the Police Department of the problem
    C. notify Control 800 on his portable radio
    D. note the problem on the back of his field patrol sheet

20. Following are three statements concerning the uniforms and personal appearance of    20.____
    enforcement agents:
        I. Dangling earrings and numerous rings are not to be worn on duty.
        II. Uniforms may be worn to and from work.
        III. A neat beard and trimmed mustache may be worn.
    *Which* of the following classifies the above statements into those which are CORRECT
    and those which are NOT?

    A. I is correct, but II and III are not
    B. II is correct, but I and III are not
    C. II and III are correct, but I is not
    D. I and III are correct, but II is not

21. Of the following, a senior enforcement agent is responsible for    21.____

    A. setting-up the weekly roll call
    B. taking portable radios for necessary repairs
    C. approving transfer requests
    D. investigating reports of lost summonses

22. Assume that a private vehicle has stopped at an unmarked crosswalk to permit a pedestrian to cross the roadway. According to the traffic regulations concerning passing, the driver of another private vehicle approaching from the rear may

    A. pass the stopped vehicle
    B. not pass the stopped vehicle
    C. pass the stopped vehicle only if weather conditions make it possible to do so safely
    D. not pass the stopped vehicle unless he does so from the left

22.____

23. A senior enforcement agent notices that some of the agents in his squad have written their rank and signature in ink on several books of summonses before they go out into the field.
    According to traffic control bureau policy, this practice is

    A. *advisable,* PRIMARILY because it saves the agents time in the field
    B. *advisable,* PRIMARILY because those summonses cannot be taken and used by other agents
    C. *inadvisable,* PRIMARILY because an agent may resign or be transferred, leaving the district office with several pre-signed summonses
    D. *inadvisable,* PRIMARILY because it wastes time in the district office

23.____

24. A senior enforcement agent notices that the uniform of one of the agents under his supervision is in such poor condition that the senior believes it should be replaced.
    According to traffic control bureau procedures, the NEXT step the senior should take is to

    A. order the agent to purchase a new uniform
    B. check to see that the agent purchases a new uniform within 10 days
    C. make a note that the agent needs a new uniform and report this fact to the district commander at the next uniform inspection
    D. ask the district commander to inspect the agent's uniform as soon as possible

24.____

25. A senior enforcement agent on patrol hears the following messages exchanged between an enforcement agent and the radio dispatcher:
    ENFORCEMENT AGENT: 10-15, New York Plate IDA MARY PETER 1 - 2 - 3 - 4, K
    DISPATCHER: 10-4, 10-6, K
    This is followed by :
    DISPATCHER: New York Plate IDA MARY PETER 1-2-3-4, 10-17, K
    ENFORCEMENT AGENT: 10-4, K
    *Which one* of the following BEST describes this exchange of messages?

    A. The agent is calling for a tow truck for a vehicle with New York license plate number IMP 1234, and the Dispatcher verifies that a tow truck is on the way
    B. The agent is requesting information on a vehicle that may be stolen and the Dispatcher responds that the vehicle is not listed as stolen
    C. The agent is requesting information on a vehicle that may be stolen and the Dispatcher responds that the vehicle is listed as stolen
    D. The agent is reporting an accident involving a vehicle with New York license plate IMP 1234, and the Dispatcher verifies that the message has been received

25.____

26. Which one of the following is the PROPER way for an agent to correct a summons on which the agent entered an incorrect license plate number?

    A. Draw a line through the incorrect number and write the correction immediately above it
    B. Issue a new, correct summons and submit the original summons with a memo reporting the mistake to the district commander
    C. Discard the summons and the stub and renumber the next summons
    D. Erase the mistake, enter the correct information, initial the correction, and complete the summons

27. When should luminous safety vests and white glbves be worn by traffic control agents who are directing traffic? Luminous safety vests

    A. should be worn only during hours of darkness, and white gloves as weather conditions dictate
    B. should be worn at all times, and white gloves only during hours of daylight
    C. should be worn only during hours of darkness, and white gloves at all times
    D. and white gloves should be worn at all times

28. According to traffic control bureau procedures, how frequently should performance evaluation reports on probationary enforcement agents be prepared by senior enforcement agents?

    A. Every sixty days during the first year of employment
    B. Once a month during the first six months of employment
    C. Twice a month during the first year of employment
    D. Every week during the first six months of employment

29. Following are three statements concerning the use of time and leave in the traffic control bureau:
    I. An employee with more than twelve latenesses in any vacation year shall be charged double time for the latenesses.
    II. Sick leave is accrued at, the rate of 1 1/2 days a month.
    III. A request tp take time off for personal business must be submitted at least five days in advance.

    Which one of the following correctly classifies the above statements into those which are CORRECT and those which are NOT?

    A. I and II are correct, but III is not
    B. II and III are correct, but I is not
    C. II is correct, but I and III are not
    D. III is correct, but I and II are not

30. Traffic signs on certain streets indicate that stopping, standing or parking regulations do NOT apply on Sundays. These regulations are also suspended on certain holidays.
    Which of the following is NOT one of these "Sunday" holidays?

    A. Election Day           B. Labor Day
    C. Independence Day       D. Memorial Day

31. When the traffic commissioner declares a state of snow emergency, NO person may operate a

   A. commercial vehicle on any street unless the vehicle is equipped with snow tires or chains
   B. vehicle in Manhattan on any cross street between 59th Street and the Battery unless the vehicle is equipped with snow tires or chains
   C. vehicle on the Brooklyn-Queens Expressway unless the vehicle is equipped with snow tires or chains
   D. taxicab on any street in the city unless the vehicle is equipped with chains

32. A traffic control agent should NOT issue a summons when a vehicle makes an illegal left turn if the vehicle is

   A. a car with MD license plates
   B. a Sanitation Department sweeper engaged in cleaning the street
   C. an official State government vehicle
   D. a limousine with diplomatic license plates

33. An enforcement agent who has been assaulted and injured calls 911 for police assistance. When the police arrive, it would be INCORRECT for the agent to

   A. let the police know he is injured and needs immediate medical attention
   B. give both his office and home address to the police
   C. notify the district office of his location and tell the office that the police have been summoned
   D. take down the name, shield number and precinct of each police officer who participates in the incident

34. The duties of a senior parking enforcement agent include all of the following EXCEPT

   A. distributing carfare to agents
   B. filing charges against agents
   C. assisting in the training of newly assigned agents
   D. sending memos directly to the assistant director of the traffic control bureau

35. A senior parking enforcement agent should advise a traffic control agent that, while on duty at an intersection, it is generally proper to do all of the following EXCEPT

   A. give brief directions to motorists stopped for a light
   B. leave the intersection to report a fire by pulling a fire alarm box
   C. monitor all calls on his radio to learn of conditions which might cause delays in his area
   D. leave the intersection for a rest break between 7:00 a.m. and 9:00 a.m.

36. The one of the following duties which is NOT normally assigned to a senior parking enforcement agent is

   A. going on car patrol
   B. approving vacation requests
   C. observing the on-the-job performance of traffic control agents
   D. dropping off and picking up parking enforcement agents at distant field assignments

37. A senior parking enforcement agent has a tire "blowout" while driving an official department motor vehicle.
All of the following are generally correct actions to take in this situation EXCEPT

   A. steering straight ahead
   B. keeping a firm grip on the steering wheel
   C. braking quickly to stop the car
   D. releasing the gas pedal

38. While driving a department motor vehicle along the highway, you feel the car pull to the right. This is LEAST likely to be a sign of possible trouble with the

   A. steering mechanism       B. wheel alignment
   C. transmission             D. tires

39. It has been suggested that a driver should expect other drivers to do the wrong thing and be ready with a plan of action to counter the other driver's errors. Following this practice can BEST be described as

   A. *advisable,* CHIEFLY because it develops a driver's skill in handling his vehicle
   B. *advisable,* CHIEFLY because it helps to avoid accidents
   C. *inadvisable,* CHIEFLY because most other drivers follow the rules of the road
   D. *inadvisable,* CHIEFLY because it takes the driver's attention away from immediate conditions

40. A senior parking enforcement agent is driving an official department motor vehicle on patrol. She notices that the red emergency light is on, indicating that the engine is overheated. She sees steam coming out from under the engine hood.
Of the following, the MOST appropriate action for the senior to take in this situation is to

   A. stop the car, open the engine hood, get a pail of cold water, and pour it over the engine
   B. stop the car, open the engine hood, remove the radiator cap, and relieve the steam pressure in the radiator
   C. stop the car, open the engine hood, wait until the car cools down, then drive it to the nearest service station
   D. continue driving the car, but take it ti the repair shops instead of continuing on patrol

# KEY (CORRECT ANSWERS)

| | | | |
|---|---|---|---|
| 1. A | 11. B | 21. B | 31. C |
| 2. C | 12. C | 22. B | 32. B |
| 3. D | 13. A | 23. C | 33. B |
| 4. B | 14. C | 24. D | 34. D |
| 5. A | 15. A | 25. B | 35. D |
| 6. A | 16. B | 26. B | 36. B |
| 7. A | 17. A | 27. D | 37. C |
| 8. A | 18. B | 28. B | 38. C |
| 9. D | 19. C | 29. D | 39. B |
| 10. B | 20. A | 30. A | 40. C |

# TEST 2

DIRECTIONS: Each question or incomplete statement is followed by several suggested answers or completions. Select the one that BEST answers the question or completes the statement. *PRINT THE LETTER OF THE CORRECT ANSWER IN THE SPACE AT THE RIGHT.*

1. Department procedures permit operation of a department motor vehicle even when there is    1.____

   A. white exhaust vapor
   B. no transmission oil
   C. overheating
   D. low oil pressure

2. Following are three statements concerning safe following distances in highway driving:    2.____
   I. When traveling at 40 miles per hour on dry pavement, allow about 80 feet between your car and the car in front of you
   II. When driving at night at any speed, you will be able to stop within the distance lighted by your car's headlights
   III. When traveling at 30 miles per hour on wet pavement, allow about 60 feet of space between your car and the car in front of you

   *Which one* of the following *correctly* classifies the above statements into those which are CORRECT and those which are NOT?

   A. I is correct, but II and III are not
   B. II is correct, but I and III are not
   C. I and II are correct, but III is not
   D. I and III are correct, but II is not

3. Following are three statements concerning driving practices at intersections:    3.____
   I. When making a right turn, place your vehicle so as to block any vehicle that might try to squeeze between you and the curb
   II. When making a left turn, have your wheels turned while waiting for traffic to clear
   III. When driving through an intersection, have you foot off the accelerator and on the brake pedal as you approach the intersection

   *Which one* of the following *correctly* classifies the above statements into those that are PROPER and those that are NOT?

   A. I and II are proper, but III is not
   B. I and III are proper, but II is not
   C. II and III are proper, but I is not
   D. I, II and III are proper

4. Following are three statements concerning pedestrians in the city:    4.____
   I. Pedestrians are permitted to stand in the road to sell merchandise to passing motorists
   II. Pedestrians under 14 years of age typically have quick reaction time, good judgment, and are seldom involved in accidents
   III. Pedestrians may not always have the legal right of way but cars must always yield the right of way to a pedestrian

   *Which one* of the following *correctly* classifies the above statements into those which are CORRECT and those which are NOT?

   A. I and II are correct, but III is not
   B. II and III are correct, but I is not
   C. II is correct, but I and III are not
   D. III is correct, but I and II are not

QUESTIONS 5 and 6.

Questions 5 and 6 are based on the information given on the report forms pictured below and on the following page.

Chart I and Chart II are parts of the Field Patrol Sheets of two Parking Enforcement Agents. They show the numbers of violations issued on a particular day. Chart III is the Tally Sheet for that day prepared by the Senior Parking Enforcement Agent from the Field Patrol Sheets of the entire squad.

Chart I

| Area or Post | TYPE OF VIOLATION | | | | | | | | | | | |
|---|---|---|---|---|---|---|---|---|---|---|---|---|
| | Mtrs | B/S | D/P | Hyd | N/S | N/Sp | Taxi | Curb | N/P | Alt | Other | Total |
| 19 | 2 | 3 | 2 | 2 | 3 | 3 | 0 | 1 | 1 | 5 | 1 | 23 |
| 21 | 4 | 0 | 2 | 0 | 1 | 2 | 2 | 0 | 5 | 9 | 1 | 26 |
| | | | | | | | | | | | | |
| | | | | | | | | | | | | |
| | | | | | | | | | | | | |
| Totals | 6 | 3 | 4 | 2 | 4 | 5 | 2 | 1 | 6 | 14 | 2 | 49 |

Date: 2/4/    Badge: 100    Signature: PEA Browne

TCB-61    Checked by _____ Date _____

Chart II

| Area or Post | TYPE OF VIOLATION | | | | | | | | | | | |
|---|---|---|---|---|---|---|---|---|---|---|---|---|
| | Mtrs | B/S | D/P | Hyd | N/S | N/Sp | Taxi | Curb | N/P | Alt | Other | Total |
| 31 | 8 | 2 | 0 | 0 | 3 | 2 | 2 | 0 | 4 | 5 | 0 | 26 |
| 33 | 7 | 0 | 1 | 2 | 3 | 1 | 2 | 0 | 6 | 3 | 0 | 25 |
| | | | | | | | | | | | | |
| | | | | | | | | | | | | |
| | | | | | | | | | | | | |
| Totals | 15 | 2 | 1 | 2 | 6 | 3 | 4 | 0 | 10 | 8 | 0 | 51 |

Date: 2/4/    Badge: 101    Signature: PEA Grey

TCB-61    Checked by _____ Date _____

Chart III

| Name | Mtrs Ptld | Mtrs | Bus Stop | Dble Park | Hyd | No Stand | No Stop | Taxi Stand | Curb | No Park | Alt Park | Other | Total |
|---|---|---|---|---|---|---|---|---|---|---|---|---|---|
| | | | | | | TRAFFIC CONTROL BUREAU SENIORS TALLY SHEET | | | | | | Enf. 23A | |
| Green | | 18 | 2 | 3 | 1 | 6 | 0 | 0 | 0 | 4 | 10 | 1 | 45 |
| Browne | | 6 | 3 | 4 | 2 | 4 | 5 | 2 | 1 | 6 | 14 | 2 | 49 |
| White | | 12 | 0 | 0 | 0 | 2 | 1 | 1 | 0 | 8 | 8 | 1 | 33 |
| Black | | 20 | 5 | 2 | 3 | 8 | 7 | 5 | 1 | 5 | 4 | 0 | 60 |
| Grey | | 15 | 2 | 1 | 2 | 9 | 3 | 4 | 0 | 10 | 8 | 0 | 51 |
| Redding | | 17 | 0 | 1 | 3 | 7 | 5 | 3 | 0 | 8 | 6 | 0 | 50 |
| TOTAL | | 88 | 12 | 11 | 11 | 36 | 21 | 15 | 2 | 41 | 50 | 4 | 288 |

5. The Senior Parking Enforcement Agent who prepared Chart III made an error in transferring the violation totals from the Field Patrol Sheets to the Seniors Tally Sheet. Which one of the following properly describes the Tally Sheet entry if this error were corrected?

   A. Parking Enforcement Agent Browne's overall total of summonses issued would be 50
   B. Parking Enforcement Agent Browne's total of summonses issued for Double-Parking violations would be 3
   C. Parking Enforcement Agent Grey's total number of summonses issued for meter violations would be 6
   D. Parking Enforcement Agent Grey's total number of summonses issued for No Standing violations would be 6

6. The parking enforcement agent who issued the MOST summonses for bus stop and taxi stand violations is

   A. Black    B. Redding    C. White    D. Browne

7. A senior parking enforcement agent is shown a copy of an "Employee's Notice of Injury" form from an Agent who has been injured while on duty. Following is part of that report:

---

5. Exact location where accident happened: One-half block West of the Northwest corner of Seventh Avenue and 34th Street (in front of 225 West 34th Street.)

6. How did accident happen? (describe fully) I slipped in the street because I didn't look where I was going.

7. Nature and extent of injury: Broken foot

8. Did you inform your superior of this accident? Yes    Date? Thursday

*Which* of the following lists ALL of the item numbers which the senior should point out to the agent as missing necessary information?

   A. 5 and 6
   B. 5, 6 and 7
   C. 5, 6 and 8
   D. 6, 7 and 8

8. For which of the following is the information recorded on the parking enforcement agent's field patrol sheets LEAST likely to be useful to a Senior Parking Enforcement Agent?

   A. Gathering evidence for use in a disciplinary action against an agent
   B. Determining whether agents have been enforcing regulations
   C. Learning which agents have the most problems dealing with the public
   D. Investigating a complaint that an agent has been absent from his post for several hours

9. Just as a parking enforcement agent has put a summons on an illegally parked car, the driver of the car comes out of a luncheonette and begins calling her names.
   Of the following, the FIRST action the agent should take in this situation is to

   A. ask the driver to apologize
   B. call for police assistance
   C. call the supervisor for assistance
   D. walk away and say nothing

10. A senior parking enforcement agent is assigned to instruct the staff of a district office on the use of a new one-page form which will be put into use next month.
    Of the following, the BEST way to teach the staff about this new form is to

    A. call a staff meeting to explain the use of the new form and find out if the agents have any questions about its use
    B. post the new form and the instructions for completing it on a bulletin board in the District Office
    C. explain the use of the new form at morning roll call just before the agents go into the field
    D. issue a written instruction booklet to each staff member

11. A person asks a traffic control agent for the address of a neighborhood restaurant and directions to it.
    If the agent is unfamiliar with the restaurant, it would generally be BEST for him to tell the person

    A. that he is sorry, but he has not heard of the restaurant and is unable to direct him
    B. to look up the restaurant's address in a telephone book and come back to the agent for exact directions
    C. to find a policeman who should be able to direct him
    D. to look up the restaurant in a telephone book and phone them for directions

12. A senior parking enforcement agent on patrol observes an agent and a motorist shouting loudly and angrily at each other. It appears that a fight might start at any moment. Of the following, it would be MOST appropriate for the senior to

    A. continue on patrol and ask the agent about the incident at the end of the tour
    B. observe the incident from a distance and allow the agent to handle this situation alone
    C. tell the agent that he will try to handle the situation himself
    D. calm the motorist by scolding the agent in front of the motorist

13. An enforcement agent reports that one of the merchants in his patrol area with whom he is quite friendly has offered him a gift as a token of thanks for keeping people from misusing the parking spaces in front of his store. The agent explains that he would probably offend the merchant by rejecting the merchandise offered.
    The senior should advise this agent

    A. *not to accept* the gift, CHIEFLY because other agents do not receive such gifts
    B. *not to accept* the gift, CHIEFLY because acceptance would violate the department code of conduct
    C. *to accept* the gift, CHIEFLY because the Department prides itself on maintaining a good relationship with neighborhood merchants
    D. *to accept* the gift, CHIEFLY because a gift is a personal matter between two friends and has nothing to do with the job

14. An enforcement agent whose performance has been generally good tells his senior that he would like to discuss some personal problems that have been interfering with his work. In this situation, it would generally be MOST appropriate for the senior to

    A. tell the agent he has not noticed any change in his work lately and that his problems cannot be too serious
    B. listen while the agent discusses his problems, but refer him for professional counseling if his problems seem serious
    C. tell the agent that it is his responsibility to solve his own personal problems
    D. ask one of the agent's close friends on the job to have a talk with him and find out the nature of the problem

15. An enforcement agent has just completed a summons for a meter violation when the driver approaches. The driver is annoyed and demands that the summons be destroyed. Of the following, *which* is the MOST appropriate response for the agent to make?

    A. "I'm extremely sorry, sir, but I'm only doing my job."
    B. "I'm supposed to enforce the regulations strictly and without exception."
    C. "Leave me alone, mister, we're not allowed to tear up tickets."
    D. "Don't you know enough to put a dime in the meter, like everyone else parked on this block?"

16. A senior enforcement agent on foot patrol is checking summbnses on parked cars. He finds a summons on which the "scheduled fine" box is not filled in. The agent who issued the summons has already left the area.
In this situation, it would be MOST appropriate for the senior to

   A. leave the summons as it is, since the motorist can find out the amount of the fine himself
   B. find the agent and tell him to return to the car, fill in the missing information, and make a notation of the error in the district office at the end of the tour
   C. fill in the correct amount of fine on the summons and make a note on the field patrol sheet to mention the error to the agent at the end of the tour
   D. have the agent write a memorandum describing the error

17. Praise by a supervisor can be an important element in motivating subordinates. Following are three statements concerning a supervisor's praise of subordinates:
   I. In order to be effective, praise must be lavish and constantly restated.
   II. Praise should be given in a manner which meets the needs of the individual subordinate.
   III. The subordinate whose work is praised should believe that the praise is earned.

   *Which* of the following correctly classifies the above statements into those that are CORRECT and those that are NOT?

   A. I is correct, but II and III are not
   B. II and III are correct, but I is not
   C. III is correct, but I and II are not
   D. I and II are correct, but III is not

18. Assume that you are a senior enforcement agent and that several of the recently appointed agents on your squad have not been adequately enforcing alternate side of the street parking regulations.
Of the following, the MOST appropriate way for you to correct this situation is to

   A. begin disciplinary proceedings against the individuals involved
   B. call a brief meeting of your squad to review the regulations and emphasize the need for strict enforcement
   C. spend more of your own patrol time issuing summonses for violations of alternate side of the street parking regulations
   D. reprimand the entire squad during Roll Call for not enforcing alternate side of the street regulations

19. A senior enforcement agent notices that although there have been several defective meters in a recently appointed agent's patrol area, the agent has not turned in any of the Univac cards used to report broken parking meters.
Of the following, it would be MOST appropriate for the senior to assume that the

   A. district office has run out of these cards
   B. agent has spent too much time loafing to locate any broken meters
   C. agent should be disciplined for not turning in these cards
   D. agent may need more training in detecting broken meters and filling out the Univac cards

20. A senior enforcement agent, upon arriving in the district office for the 7:30AM-3:30PM tour, finds that the agent assigned to cover a priority patrol area has called in sick.
Of the following, it would generally be MOST appropriate for the senior to

    A. notify the district commander that there is no coverage for the priority patrol area
    B. call in an agent who is scheduled for a regular day off to cover the priority patrol area
    C. shift the patrol assignment of another agent to the priority patrol area
    D. cover the priority area personally while out on patrol

21. Following are three statements concerning various ways of giving orders to enforcement agents:
    I. An implied order or suggestion is usually appropriate for the inexperienced agent.
    II. A polite request is less likely to upset a sensitive agent than a direct order.
    III. A direct order is usually appropriate in an emergency situation.

    Which of the following correctly classifies the above statements into those that are CORRECT and those that are NOT?

    A. I is correct, but II and III are not
    B. II and III are correct, but I is not
    C. III is correct, but I and II are not
    D. I and II are correct, but III is not

22. A senior enforcement agent on patrol observes two agents entering a bar and ordering beer when they should be on patrol.
Of the following, the *correct* procedure for the senior to follow is to

    A. note how long they remain in the bar, say nothing to them at the time, but speak to the agents when they return to the district office
    B. make no note of the incident and quietly tell the agents to leave the bar and continue their patrol duties
    C. call the District Commander immediately to report the incident, and tell the agents to proceed directly to the district office
    D. tell the agents to return to duty, enter the incident on his field patrol sheet and on theirs, and submit a memo to the District Commander at the end of the tour

23. A senior enforcement agent feels that he is about to lose his temper while reprimanding a subordinate.
Of the following, the BEST action for the senior to take is to

    A. postpone the reprimand for a short time until his self-control is assured
    B. continue the reprimand because a loss of temper by the senior will show the subordinate the seriousness of the error he made
    C. continue the reprimand because failure to do so will show that the senior does not have complete self-control
    D. postpone the reprimand until the subordinate is capable of understanding the reason for the supervisor's loss of temper

24. Daily inspections by senior enforcement agents of their subordinates' uniforms are useful *chiefly* because

    A. they show the department that the seniors are performing their duties
    B. subordinates learn to expect the inspections and follow the rules automatically
    C. they help to insure the proper appearance of the agents before the public
    D. subordinates appreciate the attention they receive form their superiors

25. While in the field, an enforcement agent asks a senior a question about how to request maternity leave from the Department of Traffic. The senior does not know the answer.
    Of the following, it would be BEST for the senior to tell the agent

    A. to wait until she is ready to leave before inquiring about maternity leave
    B. that he does not know the answer but will get the information for her as soon as possible
    C. to call the District Commander from the field
    D. to write to her union representative

26. Enforcement agent Jones tells a senior enforcement agent that agent Smith has been taking lunch breaks of up to two hours.
    Of the following, the FIRST thing for the senior to do in this situation is to

    A. tell agent Jones to stop gossiping about her fellow employees
    B. refer the matter to the District Commander for investigation
    C. take disciplinary action against agent Smith
    D. investigate the matter and get all the facts from both agents

27. During their probationary period, parking enforcement and traffic control agents are informed of deficiencies in their performance.
    This practice is

    A. *good,* chiefly because agents learn where they need to improve
    B. *good,* chiefly because agents can defend themselves against false charges
    C. *poor,* chiefly because agents may become easily discouraged
    D. *poor,* chiefly because any improvement in performance is likely to be temporary

28. Of the following, the MOST practical method of providing on-the-job training for newly assigned enforcement agents who have just completed the course at the training division is for the senior to

    A. assign each new agent to go out on patrol with a more experienced agent until the new agent learns the job
    B. have the new agents accompany the senior on patrol for about two weeks
    C. accompany the new agents on patrol for the first half of their tour each day, but let them patrol on their own for the last half
    D. give each agent his own patrol area to cover alone, thus letting him learn the job by doing it

29. A senior enforcement agent should generally give an *oral* order rather than a *written* order to subordinates when

    A. a precise record of the instructions given in the order is required
    B. the subordinates must refresh their memories from time to time to properly carry out the order

C. the order is a very complicated one
D. the order involves a routine activity which the subordinates have performed properly in the past

30. The one of the following which is NOT a valid principle for a supervisor to keep in mind when talking to a subordinate about his performance is:

    A. People frequently know when they deserve criticism
    B. Supervisors should be prepared to offer suggestions to subordinates about how to improve their work
    C. Good points should be discussed before bad points
    D. Magnifying a subordinate's faults will get him to improve faster

31. In many organizations information travels quickly through the "grapevine".
    Following are three statements concerning the "grapevine":
    I. Information an enforcement agent does not want to tell her supervisor may reach the supervisor through the grapevine.
    II. A supervisor can often do her job better by knowing the information that travels through the grapevine.
    III. A supervisor can depend on the grapevine as a way to get accurate information from the enforcement agents on her staff.

    Which one of the following correctly classifies the above statements into those which are generally CORRECT and those which are NOT?

    A. II is correct, but I and III are not
    B. III is correct, but I and II are not
    C. I and II are correct, but III is not
    D. I and III are correct, but II is not

32. The Traffic Control Bureau has received a letter of complaint from a member of the public about an enforcement agent. Preliminary investigation shows that the complaint appears to be unjustified and that the subordinate is completely innocent.
    Of the following, it would generally be MOST appropriate for the agent's supervisor to

    A. proceed no further since the complaint is unjustified
    B. transfer the subordinate to another patrol assignment to prevent possible contact with the same member of the public
    C. make no note of the complaint on a complaint record form because any entry in the files could harm the subordinate's career
    D. complete a thorough investigation of the matter and fill out a complaint record form

33. Following are three statements concerning supervision:
    I. A supervisor knows he is doing a good job if his subordinates depend upon him to make every decision
    II. A supervisor who delegates authority to his subordinates soon finds that his subordinates begin to resent him.
    III. Giving credit for good work is frequently an effective method of getting subordinates to work harder.

    Which one of the following correctly classifies the above statements into those that are CORRECT and those that are NOT?

    A. I and II are correct, but III is not
    B. II and III are correct, but I is not

C. II is correct, but I and III are not
D. III is correct, but I and II are not

34. Preparing supervisors to carry out their training responsibilities is the most effective training activity that can be carried on.
Applying this principle to senior enforcement agents would be

   A. *undesirable,* chiefly because adequate training is given to all enforcement agents at the training division
   B. *undesirable,* chiefly because training supervisors is costly and inefficient
   C. *desirable,* chiefly because training of subordinates by supervisors who are trained to teach is generaly helpful
   D. *desirable,* chiefly because it gives the seniors an added job function

35. Training senior enforcement agents to take over the job of the District Commander when the District Commander is absent is *generally*

   A. *desirable*, chiefly because it increases staff flexibility and the district's readiness to handle emergencies
   B. *desirable*, chiefly because it enables seniors to pass promotion examinations
   C. *undesirable*, chiefly because errors made by the seniors during such training cannot be corrected
   D. *undesirable,* chiefly because Department of Traffic regulations forbid seniors from performing the District Commander's job

36. Following are three statements concerning on-the-job training:
   I. On-the-job training is rarely used as a method of training employees.
   II. On-the-job training is often carried on with little or no planning.
   III. On-the-job training is often less expensive than other types of training.

   Which one of the following BEST classifies the above statements into those that are CORRECT and those that are NOT?

   A. I is correct, but II and III are not
   B. II is correct, but I and III are not
   C. I and II are correct, but III is not
   D. II and III are correct, but I is not

37. The one of the following that is the MOST appropriate action for a senior enforcement agent to take when criticizing a subordinate for carelessness in making out summonses is to

   A. make the subordinate feel ashamed of his work
   B. direct his criticism at specific mistakes made by the subordinate
   C. focus his comments on the subordinate's overall job performance
   D. tell the subordinate that his carelessness shows that he is unable to handle the job

38. Of the following, the LEAST appropriate action for a supervisor to take in preparing a disciplinary case against a subordinate is to

    A. keep careful records of each incident in which the subordinate has been guilty of misconduct or incompetency, even though immediate disciplinary action may not be necessary
    B. discuss with the employee each incident of misconduct as it occurs so the employee knows where he stands
    C. accept memoranda from any other employees who may have been witnesses to acts of misconduct
    D. keep the subordinate's personnel file confidential so that he is unaware of the evidence being gathered against him

38._____

39. Traffic control agents on duty at intersections should be instructed by their supervisors to do all of the following EXCEPT

    A. stand in the center of the intersection of two-way streets
    B. turn in the direction in which traffic is moving
    C. direct turning vehicles to complete their turns behind him
    D. move from place to place within an intersection of a one-way street, as traffic conditions change

39._____

40. The one of the following which is NOT an acceptable reason for taking disciplinary action against a subordinate guilty of serious violations of the rules is that

    A. the supervisor can "let off steam" against subordinates who break rules frequently
    B. a subordinate whose work continues to be unsatisfactory may be terminated
    C. a subordinate may be encouraged to improve his work
    D. an example is set for other employees

40._____

## KEY (CORRECT ANSWERS)

| | | | | | | | |
|---|---|---|---|---|---|---|---|
| 1. | A | 11. | B | 21. | B | 31. | C |
| 2. | A | 12. | C | 22. | D | 32. | D |
| 3. | B | 13. | B | 23. | A | 33. | D |
| 4. | D | 14. | B | 24. | C | 34. | C |
| 5. | D | 15. | B | 25. | B | 35. | A |
| 6. | A | 16. | C | 26. | D | 36. | D |
| 7. | D | 17. | B | 27. | A | 37. | B |
| 8. | C | 18. | B | 28. | A | 38. | D |
| 9. | D | 19. | D | 29. | D | 39. | C |
| 10. | A | 20. | C | 30. | D | 40. | A |

# EXAMINATION SECTION
## TEST 1

DIRECTIONS: Each question or incomplete statement is followed by several suggested answers or completions. Select the one that BEST answers the question or completes the statement. *PRINT THE LETTER OF THE CORRECT ANSWER IN THE SPACE AT THE RIGHT.*

1. Fires of flammable liquids and greases which can be extinguished by blanketing or smothering are classified as Class _____ fires.

    A. *A*  B. *B*  C. *C*  D. *D*

2. Of the following pieces of safety equipment issued by the Division of Safety, Department of Sanitation, the ones which are NOT for the use of men working at incinerators are

    A. reflector strips
    B. safety belts
    C. colored goggles
    D. wooden sandals

3. A *compound* bone fracture can be recognized by the fact that

    A. more than one bone is broken
    B. the bone is broken in more than one place
    C. the skin is broken as well as the bone at the place of impact
    D. the bone is broken into small pieces

4. Of the following, the MOST likely cause of broken tire sidewalls is

    A. a punctured tire belt
    B. sudden starts and stops
    C. under-inflation of tires
    D. over-inflation of tires

5. If an accident victim must be treated for shock, he should be kept warm and placed in *shock position*.
   Placed in *shock position refers* to

    A. shifting the weight of a third-degree burn victim so that he supports the weight on unburned regions of his body
    B. positioning the victim's body horizontally or slightly tilted with chest and head lower than the feet
    C. giving the victim the support necessary for him to sit in an upright position
    D. sitting the victim in a chair and placing his head between his knees

6. A method of controlling bleeding from an arm that should be used ONLY in the most serious cases is

    A. digital pressure
    B. direct pressure
    C. coagulation
    D. a tourniquet

7. A symptom of shock in an accident victim is

    A. perspiration on upper lip and forehead
    B. very rapid pulse
    C. lack of perspiration
    D. abdominal cramps

8. Assume that you notice a new sanitation man using his hands to stuff overflow trash back into the hopper of a collection truck while its compactor is in operation. Your FIRST action should be to

   A. tell the driver of the truck to stop the compactor
   B. assign the man to another job
   C. stop the man
   D. get witnesses so that you can prepare disciplinary charges against the man

9. One of the methods being used by the Department of Sanitation to reduce the numbers of motor vehicle accidents is

   A. putting a second man in all trucks driven by accident repeaters
   B. stopping all accident repeaters from driving again
   C. establishing a defensive driving course for all accident repeaters
   D. attaching special governors to the engine of vehicles driven by all accident repeaters

10. An example of an important land reclamation (landfill) is

    A. Ferry Point Park, Bronx
    B. Cunningham Park, Queens
    C. Clove Lakes Park, Staten Island
    D. Prospect Park, Brooklyn

11. The number of Borough Commands in the Bureau of Cleaning and Collection is

    A. 58    B. 22    C. 11    D. 6

12. At a waste disposal location, a vehicle operator can offer no proof that his vehicle qualifies for dumping. The operator refuses to accept the decision of the officer-in-charge that he must leave.
    Of the following, the BEST response for the officer-in-charge would be to

    A. inform the operator that the police will be called, and then call them
    B. contact the Bureau Operations Office for advice
    C. issue a voluntary load ticket
    D. allow the dumping, but include a complete description of the incident in the daily report

13. The officer-in-charge at a Marine Transfer Station must *sound* a barge upon its arrival at the station.
    The purpose of *sounding* the barge is to

    A. act as a signal to the station's crew
    B. determine the degree of *list* or *trim*
    C. check for undisposed refuse
    D. measure the water depth

14. Of all the methods of final waste disposal used by the Department, the one which accounts for the GREATEST amount of waste material is   14.____

    A. dumping at sanitary landfills
    B. incinerating in city-owned plants
    C. transferring refuse by barge to be dumped at sea
    D. reprocessing refuse into reusable materials

15. The MAIN purpose of using water with a mechanical broom is to   15.____

    A. flush the dirt toward the broom
    B. hold the dust down
    C. prevent sticking of the dirt to the machine parts
    D. lubricate the shaft of the broom

16. Mechanical brooms have dual controls in order to   16.____

    A. allow two operators to work simultaneously
    B. permit the operator to take a driving position nearest the curb
    C. permit the operator to use either his right or left hand
    D. substitute for one set of controls when driving if the other becomes inoperable

17. An area in which manual sweepers are STILL generally required is the   17.____

    A. light vehicular traffic area
    B. light pedestrian traffic area
    C. lot area
    D. commercial area with heavy traffic

18. The roll-on, roll-off container used by the Department of Sanitation has a cubic yard capacity of _____ cubic yards.   18.____

    A. 29     B. 39     C. 49     D. 59

19. The Auxiliary Field Force would be summoned to remove   19.____

    A. ash cans left outside of public buildings
    B. Class A trade wastes
    C. large dead animals
    D. litter baskets located in heavily trafficked pedestrian areas

20. Private cartmen are required to obtain Class 4 permits in order to transport   20.____

    A. ashes or manure          B. dead animals
    C. night soil               D. swill

21. The one of the following which is NOT a division of the Bureau of Waste Disposal is the _____ Division.   21.____

    A. Incinerator              B. Landfill
    C. Marine Unloading         D. Snow Disposal

22. Furnace temperatures in an incinerator NORMALLY range from _____ to _____ degrees   22.____

    A. 900; 1300   B. 1400; 1800   C. 1900; 2300   D. 2400; 2800

23. The six waste disposal plants in New York City have a total daily rated capacity of APPROXIMATELY _____ tons.

   A. 3,500   B. 6,000   C. 7,200   D. 9,300

24. The electrostatic precipitator at an incinerator is used to

   A. control air pollution
   B. gravity feed refuse into the hopper
   C. prevent serious electric shocks
   D. quench troughs

25. The hours for which Class A streets in the alternate side parking program are restricted for parking are BETWEEN

   A. 4 A.M. to 7 A.M., or 9 A.M. to 1 P.M.
   B. 6 A.M. to 9 A.M., or 9 A.M. to 11 A.M.
   C. 8 A.M. to 11 A.M., or 11 A.M. to 2 P.M.
   D. 10 A.M. to 12 Noon, or 12 Noon to 3 P.M.

26. The areas in which Class B streets are PREDOMINANTLY located are _____ areas.

   A. business           B. low traffic
   C. metered            D. outlying

27. Litter baskets in a heavy pedestrian traffic area should be placed no further apart than EVERY _____ feet with a minimum of 3 per block over _____ feet in length.

   A. 50; 50   B. 75; 75   C. 100; 100   D. 125; 125

28. The USUAL time for cleaning most metered areas in the street is

   A. immediately after the parking restriction is removed
   B. any time during the night
   C. any time between 7:00 P.M. and 8:00 A.M.
   D. one hour before the metered parking goes into effect

29. The three MAIN components of the *machine flusher* are the tank,

   A. pump, and hopper           B. hopper, and spraybar
   C. pump, and spray system     D. hopper, and gutter broom

30. A panscraper would be used for

   A. clearing roadways and streets of encumbrances
   B. rough cleaning and piling of street dirt
   C. scraping dirt off litter cans
   D. sweeping dirt onto a scoop shovel

31. A piece of equipment that is NOT used for plowing, piling, sewering, or scattering in snow operations is the

   A. bulldozer              B. crane with dragline
   C. front end loader       D. spreader with a V plow

32. The size of a type A container used with a unit hoist is _____ cubic yards. 32.____
    A. 6        B. 8        C. 10        D. 12

33. The capacity of the *escalator* or *batch compactor* truck generally used by the Department of Sanitation is MOST NEARLY _____ cubic yards. 33.____
    A. 11       B. 20       C. 26        D. 35

34. The average capacity, in gallons, of a tank truck used by the Department of Sanitation is MOST NEARLY _____ gallons. 34.____
    A. 2,000    B. 2,500    C. 3,000     D. 3,500

35. Although some active Marine Transfer Stations may load more barges, the number of barges loaded daily by the average Marine Transfer Station is 35.____
    A. 2        B. 5        C. 8         D. 11

# KEY (CORRECT ANSWERS)

| | | | |
|---|---|---|---|
| 1. B | | 16. B | |
| 2. A | | 17. D | |
| 3. C | | 18. B | |
| 4. C | | 19. C | |
| 5. B | | 20. B | |
| 6. D | | 21. D | |
| 7. A | | 22. B | |
| 8. C | | 23. B | |
| 9. C | | 24. A | |
| 10. A | | 25. C | |
| 11. C | | 26. A | |
| 12. B | | 27. C | |
| 13. D | | 28. D | |
| 14. A | | 29. C | |
| 15. B | | 30. B | |

31. B
32. D
33. B
34. B
35. A

# TEST 2

DIRECTIONS: Each question or incomplete statement is followed by several suggested answers or completions. Select the one that BEST answers the question or completes the statement. *PRINT THE LETTER OF THE CORRECT ANSWER IN THE SPACE AT THE RIGHT.*

1. Athey wagons are used by the Marine Unloading Division PRIMARILY to

    A. haul material from unloading plants to the edge of the active fill
    B. assist in towing operations in the vicinity of unloading plants
    C. temporarily hold refuse brought in by collection trucks while an empty barge is being prepared
    D. collect refuse which spills into the water during the unloading of a barge

1.\_\_\_\_

2. At present, the method used to bring barges to the Marine Transfer Station is

    A. by Department of Sanitation tugboats only
    B. by chartered tugboats only
    C. either under their own power or by chartered tugboats
    D. by both Department of Sanitation and chartered tugboats

2.\_\_\_\_

3. At Marine Transfer Stations, trucked waste is dumped onto barges which are then towed to the final disposal point located at

    A. the old Brooklyn Navy Yard
    B. Marine Park, Brooklyn
    C. Hunts Point, Bronx
    D. Fresh Kills, Staten Island

3.\_\_\_\_

4. In the Department of Sanitation's Preventive Maintenance Program, Class *A* maintenance of motor vehicles includes

    A. tune-up of engine
    B. daily inspection of oil level
    C. six-week lubrication
    D. 50,000 mile or yearly major overhaul by shop mechanics

4.\_\_\_\_

5. Of the following items, the one which would NOT usually appear on the special shift ticket for Mechanical Broom Activities is

    A. class of streets swept *(A, B, or C)*
    B. location of dumping point
    C. total curb miles swept
    D. weight of street dirt collected

5.\_\_\_\_

6. If, in the course of collection on his assigned route, a sanitation man collects *trade-waste,* he is

    A. violating the Code of Discipline
    B. violating the Code of Discipline if he has not determined its source before removing it
    C. violating the Code of Discipline if the trade waste is also not an encumberance
    D. not violating the Code of Discipline

6.\_\_\_\_

7. When a foreman assists in the registration of emergency laborers for snow removal, he must obtain from each laborer

   A. two unmounted photographs
   B. documentary proof of U.S. citizenship
   C. a sworn statement indicating that his religion does not forbid working on Saturdays or Sundays
   D. valid working papers

8. The relationship of the administrator of EPA and the Mayor is organizationally MOST similar to that of a foreman and

   A. a District Superintendent
   B. a General Superintendent
   C. the Sanitation Commissioner
   D. a sanitation man

9. The three agencies which make up the Environmental Protection Administration are the Departments of _____ and Sanitation.

   A. Sewage Disposal, Water Purification,
   B. Air Resources, Water Resources,
   C. Water Resources, Sewage Disposal,
   D. Air Resources, Sewage Disposal,

10. The Division that is responsible for all investigations of a special or confidential nature within the Environmental Protection Agency is the Division of

    A. Enforcement          B. Inquiry
    C. Investigation        D. Prosecution

11. The regulations of the Department of Sanitation state that hydrants are NOT to be used in the winter when the temperatures are _____ degrees or lower.

    A. 34          B. 38          C. 42          D. 45

12. Approximately what percentage of the refuse handled by the Bureau of Waste Disposal is processed by the Incinerator Division? _____ percent.

    A. 5           B. 20          C. 35          D. 50

13. The one of the following functions that is performed by the Division of Office Service and Permits is

    A. insuring that employees are utilizing sick leave for its intended purpose
    B. issuing and controlling tare keys used in electronic weighing of loads
    C. maintaining records for pensioners
    D. preparing, publishing, and distributing monthly progress reports and statistical review

14. The Commissioner of the Department of Sanitation is appointed by the

    A. Deputy Administrator of EPA      B. City Council
    C. Administrator of EPA             D. Mayor

15. The approximate number of sanitation personnel in the Bureau of Cleaning and Collection is _____ persons.  15.____

    A. 7,000  B. 6,000  C. 11,000  D. 25,000

16. The total number of miles of expressways and parkways in New York City is MOST NEARLY _____ miles.  16.____

    A. 375  B. 550  C. 825  D. 1500

17. The regular collection schedule for outlying residential areas is _____ time(s) a week.  17.____

    A. one  
    B. two or three  
    C. four or five  
    D. six or seven

18. In the Borough of Manhattan, if a snowfall stops at 10 A.M., the time by which the owner of a building must have the snow removed from the sidewalk in front of the building is  18.____

    A. noon  B. 2P.M.  C. 4P.M.  D. 6P.M.

19. If ice is frozen solid and cannot be removed without damaging the pavement in front of a building, the owner of the building MUST clean the sidewalk in front of the building  19.____

    A. as soon as the weather permits
    B. at the convenience of the owner
    C. as soon as possible, even if the sidewalk becomes damaged in the process
    D. only if he has tried using salt first and it has not melted the ice

20. An owner of a building must provide separate receptacles for all of the following types of waste EXCEPT  20.____

    A. ashes  B. liquid waste  C. sand  D. refuse

21. The receptacles for garbage must be large enough and in sufficient quantity to contain the garbage that would accumulate in the building for a period of _____ hours.  21.____

    A. 15  B. 30  C. 45  D. 60

22. According to the New York City Health Code, after the sanitation man has emptied the contents of a garbage receptacle, the receptacle must be  22.____

    A. removed immediately from the front of the building by the owner
    B. covered by the owner, but may remain in front of the building for no more than two hours
    C. removed from the front of the building within two hours by the owner
    D. covered immediately by the owner

23. According to the New York City Health Code, the preferred method of leaving newspapers for collection is  23.____

    A. putting available light refuse on top of a bundle of papers to weight them down
    B. putting the papers in a separate barrel
    C. securely tieing the bundle of papers
    D. stacking the papers under the garbage receptacle

24. According to the New York City Health Code, the sharing of receptacles for garbage in a light residential area is    24._____

    A. *permitted* only when the buildings are one-family dwellings
    B. *permitted* only when the receptacles are of heavy metal construction
    C. *permitted* only when there is insufficient daily waste to fill more than one receptacle
    D. *not permitted*

25. The possible punishment under the Administrative Code if a homeowner prevents a sanitation man from sweeping the street in front of the homeowner's house is    25._____

    A. a fine of not more than $25, or imprisonment for 10 days or less, or both
    B. a verbal reprimand from the sanitation man, and a written reprimand from the Supervisor
    C. imprisonment for at least 20 days
    D. a fine of not less than $100

26. The unit that may issue summonses for infractions of law is the _____ unit.    26._____

    A. public service         B. disposable waste
    C. inspectional force     D. health control

27. An owner of a one-family house rents the house, through a managing agent, to an individual family living alone in the house.    27._____
    According to the New York City Health Code, the person or persons responsible for keeping the sidewalk in front of the house clean is

    A. the tenant, the agent, and the owner
    B. *only* the tenant and the owner
    C. *only* the tenant and the agent
    D. *only* the tenant

28. The Public Relations Office's budget for a Sanitation Unit was $100,000 in 2002. Their 2003 budget was 5% higher than that of 2002, and their 2004 budget was 10% higher than that of 2003.    28._____
    The Office's budget for 2004 is

    A. $105,500    B. $111,500    C. $115,500    D. $120,500

29. The City recently purchased three pieces of machinery for use at a sanitation garage. One machine cost $1,739.55, the second machine cost $6,284.00. The total cost for all three machines was $12,721.00.    29._____
    How much did the THIRD machine cost?

    A. $4,607.55    B. $4,697.45    C. $4,797.55    D. $4,798.45

30. An Emergency Sanitation Aide is paid at the rate of $14.40 per hour. He worked 45 hours in one week and was paid double time for 3 of the 45 hours worked during this week.    30._____
    What was his TOTAL gross earnings for the week?

    A. $673.80    B. $691.20    C. $757.80    D. $931.20

31. The one of the following words that has the OPPOSITE meaning of *flammable* is  31.____

   A. burnable
   B. inflammable
   C. combustible
   D. nonflammable

32. The one of the following words that is spelled CORRECTLY is  32.____

   A. maintainance
   B. maintenence
   C. maintainence
   D. maintenance

33. The one of the following words that is spelled CORRECTLY is  33.____

   A. comparable
   B. comprable
   C. comparible
   D. commparable

34. The one of the following words that has the OPPOSITE meaning of *adversary* is  34.____

   A. enemy   B. ally   C. opponent   D. foe

35. The one of the following words that is spelled CORRECTLY is  35.____

   A. harassment
   B. harrasment
   C. harasment
   D. harrassment

---

## KEY (CORRECT ANSWERS)

| | | | |
|---|---|---|---|
| 1. A | | 16. B | |
| 2. B | | 17. B | |
| 3. D | | 18. B | |
| 4. B | | 19. A | |
| 5. D | | 20. C | |
| 6. A | | 21. D | |
| 7. A | | 22. A | |
| 8. A | | 23. C | |
| 9. B | | 24. D | |
| 10. A | | 25. A | |
| 11. A | | 26. C | |
| 12. B | | 27. A | |
| 13. B | | 28. C | |
| 14. D | | 29. B | |
| 15. C | | 30. B | |

31. D
32. D
33. A
34. B
35. A

# MAP READING
# EXAMINATION SECTION
# TEST 1

DIRECTIONS: Each question or incomplete statement is followed by several suggested answers or completions. Select the one that BEST answers the question or completes the Statement. *PRINT THE LETTER OF THE CORRECT ANSWER IN THE SPACE AT THE RIGHT.*

Questions 1-5.

DIRECTIONS: Questions 1 through 5 are to be answered SOLELY on the basis of the following information and map.

An employee may be required to assist civilians who seek travel directions or referral to city agencies and facilities.

The following is a map of part of a city, where several public offices and other institutions are located. Each of the squares represents one city block. Street names are as shown. If there is an arrow next to the street name, it means the street is one-way only in the direction of the arrow. If there is no arrow next to the street name, two-way traffic is allowed.

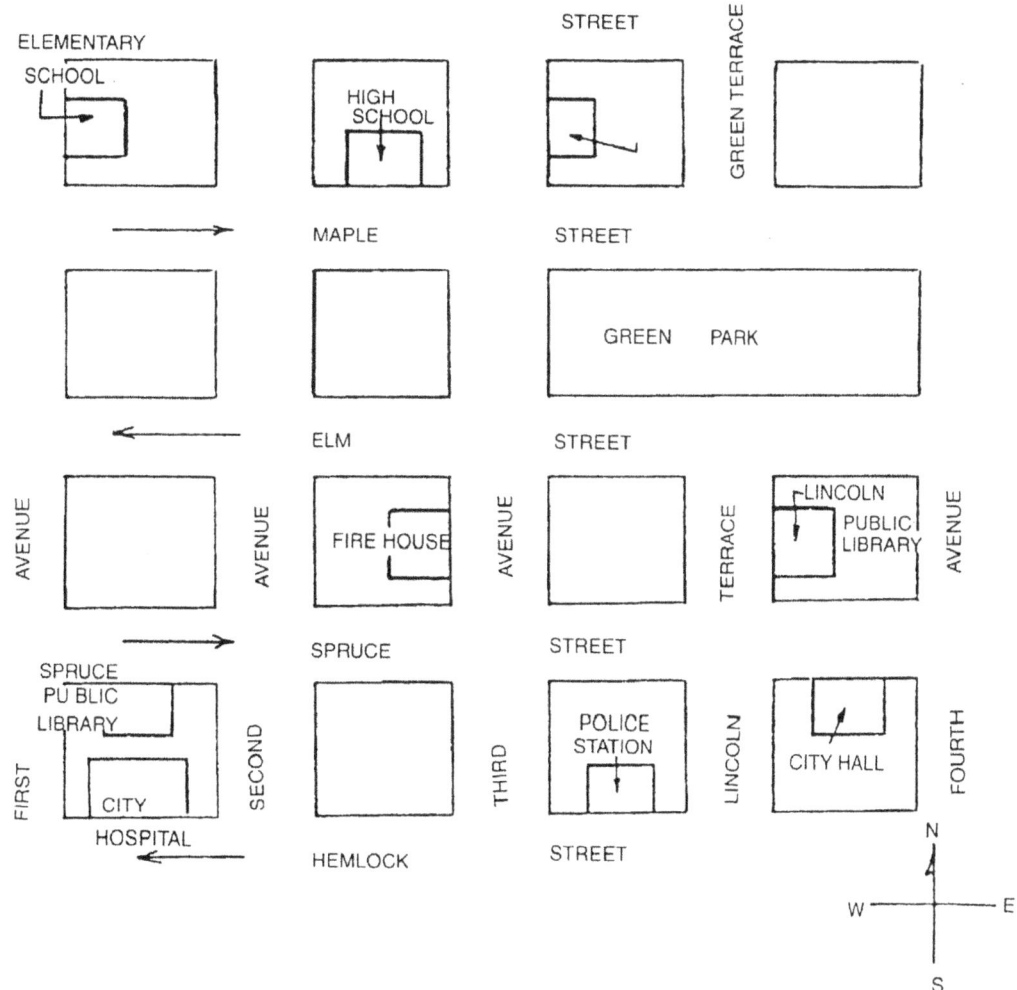

1. A woman whose handbag was stolen from her in Green Park asks a firefighter at the fire-house where to go to report the crime.
   The firefighter should tell the woman to go to the

   A. police station on Spruce Street
   B. police station on Hemlock Street
   C. city hall on Spruce Street
   D. city hall on Hemlock Street

2. A disabled senior citizen who lives on Green Terrace telephones the firehouse to ask which library is closest to her home.
   The firefighter should tell the senior citizen it is the

   A. Spruce Public Library on Lincoln Terrace
   B. Lincoln Public Library on Spruce Street
   C. Spruce Public Library on Spruce Street
   D. Lincoln Public Library on Lincoln Terrace

3. A woman calls the firehouse to ask for the exact location of City Hall.
   She should be told that it is on

   A. Hemlock Street, between Lincoln Terrace and Fourth Avenue
   B. Spruce Street, between Lincoln Terrace and Fourth Avenue
   C. Lincoln Terrace, between Spruce Street and Elm Street
   D. Green Terrace, between Maple Street and Pine Street

4. A delivery truck driver is having trouble finding the high school to make a delivery. The driver parks the truck across from the firehouse on Third Avenue facing north and goes into the firehouse to ask directions.
   In giving directions, the firefighter should tell the driver to go _____ to the school.

   A. north on Third Avenue to Pine Street and then make a right
   B. south on Third Avenue, make a left on Hemlock Street, and then make a right on Second Avenue
   C. north on Third Avenue, turn left on Elm Street, make a right on Second Avenue and go to Maple Street, then make another right
   D. north on Third Avenue to Maple Street, and then make a left

5. A man comes to the firehouse accompanied by his son and daughter. He wants to register his son in the high school and his daughter in the elementary school. He asks a firefighter which school is closest for him to walk to from the firehouse.
   The firefighter should tell the man that the

   A. high school is closer than the elementary school
   B. elementary school is closer than the high school
   C. elementary school and high school are the same distance away
   D. elementary school and high school are in opposite directions

Questions 6-8.

DIRECTIONS: Questions 6 through 8 are to be answered SOLELY on the basis of the following map and information. The flow of traffic is indicated by the arrows. If there is only one arrow shown, then traffic flows in the direction indicated by the arrow. If there are two arrows, then traffic flows in both directions. You must follow the flow of traffic

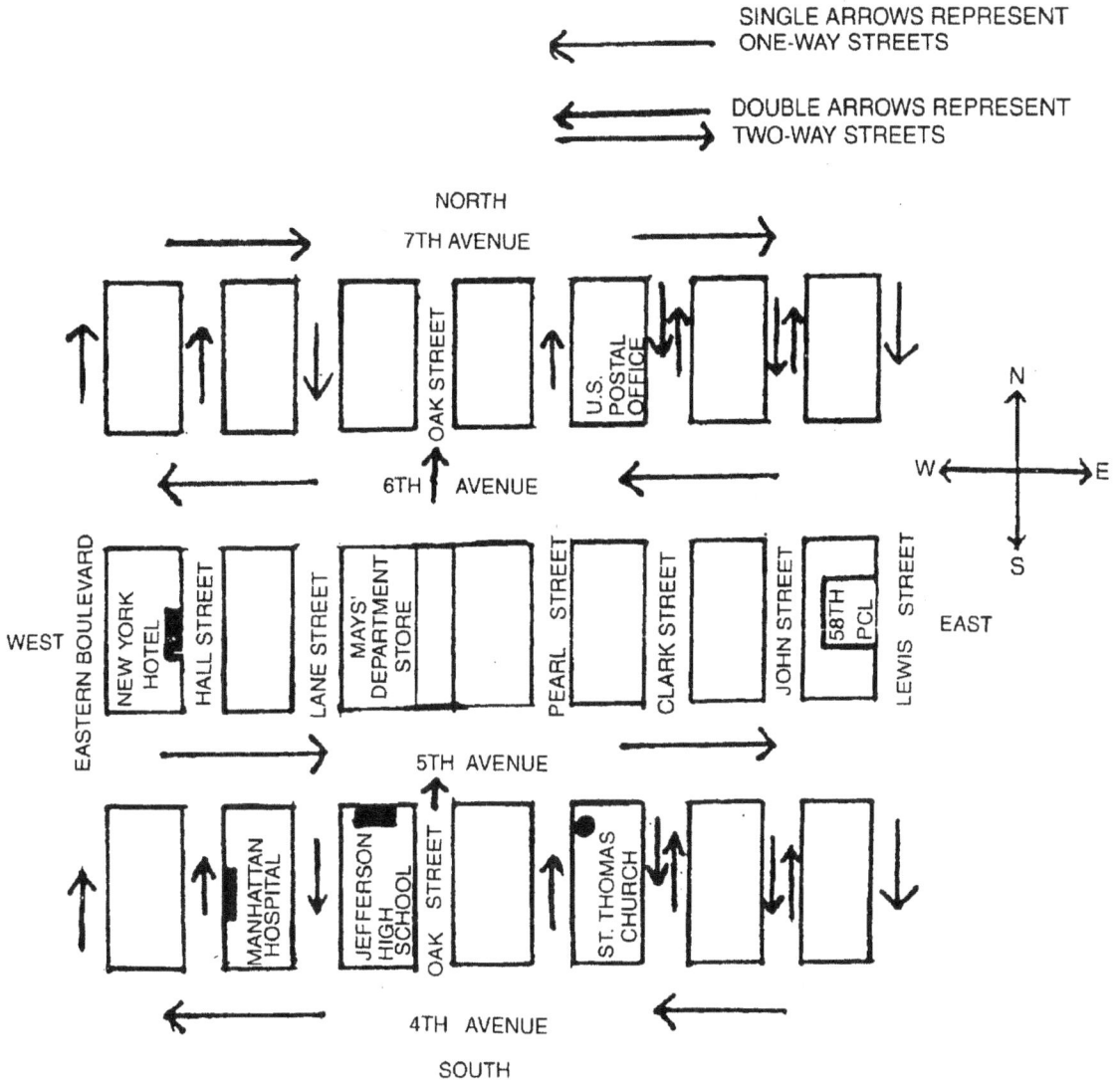

6. Traffic Enforcement Agent Fox was on foot patrol at John Street between 6th and 7th Avenues when a motorist driving southbound asked her for directions to the New York Hotel, which is located on Hall Street between 5th and 6th Avenues. Which one of the following is the SHORTEST route for Agent Fox to direct the motorist to take, making sure to obey all traffic regulations?
Travel _____ to the New York Hotel.

   A. north on John Street, then east on 7th Avenue, then north on Lewis Street, then west on 4th Avenue, then north on Eastern Boulevard, then east on 5th Avenue, then north on Hall Street
   B. south on John Street, then west on 6th Avenue, then south on Eastern Boulevard, then east on 5th Avenue, then north on Hall Street

C. south on John Street, then west on 6th Avenue, then south on Clark Street, then east on 4th Avenue, then north on Eastern Boulevard, then east on 5th Avenue, then north on Hall Street
D. south on John Street, then west on 4th Avenue, then north on Hall Street

7. Traffic Enforcement Agent Murphy is on motorized patrol on 7th Avenue between Oak Street and Pearl Street when Lt. Robertson radios him to go to Jefferson High School, located on 5th Avenue between Lane Street and Oak Street. Which one of the following is the SHORTEST route for Agent Murphy to take, making sure to obey all the traffic regulations?
Travel east on 7th Avenue, then south on _____, then east on 5th Avenue to Jefferson High School.

   A. Clark Street, then west on 4th Avenue, then north on Hall Street
   B. Pearl Street, then west on 4th Avenue, then north on Lane Street
   C. Lewis Street, then west on 6th Avenue, then south on Hall Street
   D. Lewis Street, then west on 4th Avenue, then north on Oak Street

8. Traffic Enforcement Agent Vasquez was on 4th Avenue and Eastern Boulevard when a motorist asked him for directions to the 58th Police Precinct, which is located on Lewis Street between 5th and 6th Avenues.
Which one of the following is the SHORTEST route for Agent Vasquez to direct the motorist to take, making sure to obey all traffic regulations.
Travel north on Eastern Boulevard, then east on _____ on Lewis Street to the 58th Police Precinct.

   A. 5th Avenue, then north
   B. 7th Avenue, then south
   C. 6th Avenue, then north on Pearl Street, then east on 7th Avenue, then south
   D. 5th Avenue, then north on Clark Street, then east on 6th Avenue, then south

Questions 9-13.

DIRECTIONS: Questions 9 through 13 are to be answered SOLELY on the basis of the following map and the following information.

Toll collectors answer motorists' questions concerning directions by reading a map of the metropolitan area. Although many alternate routes leading to destinations exist on the following map, you are to choose the MOST direct route of those given.

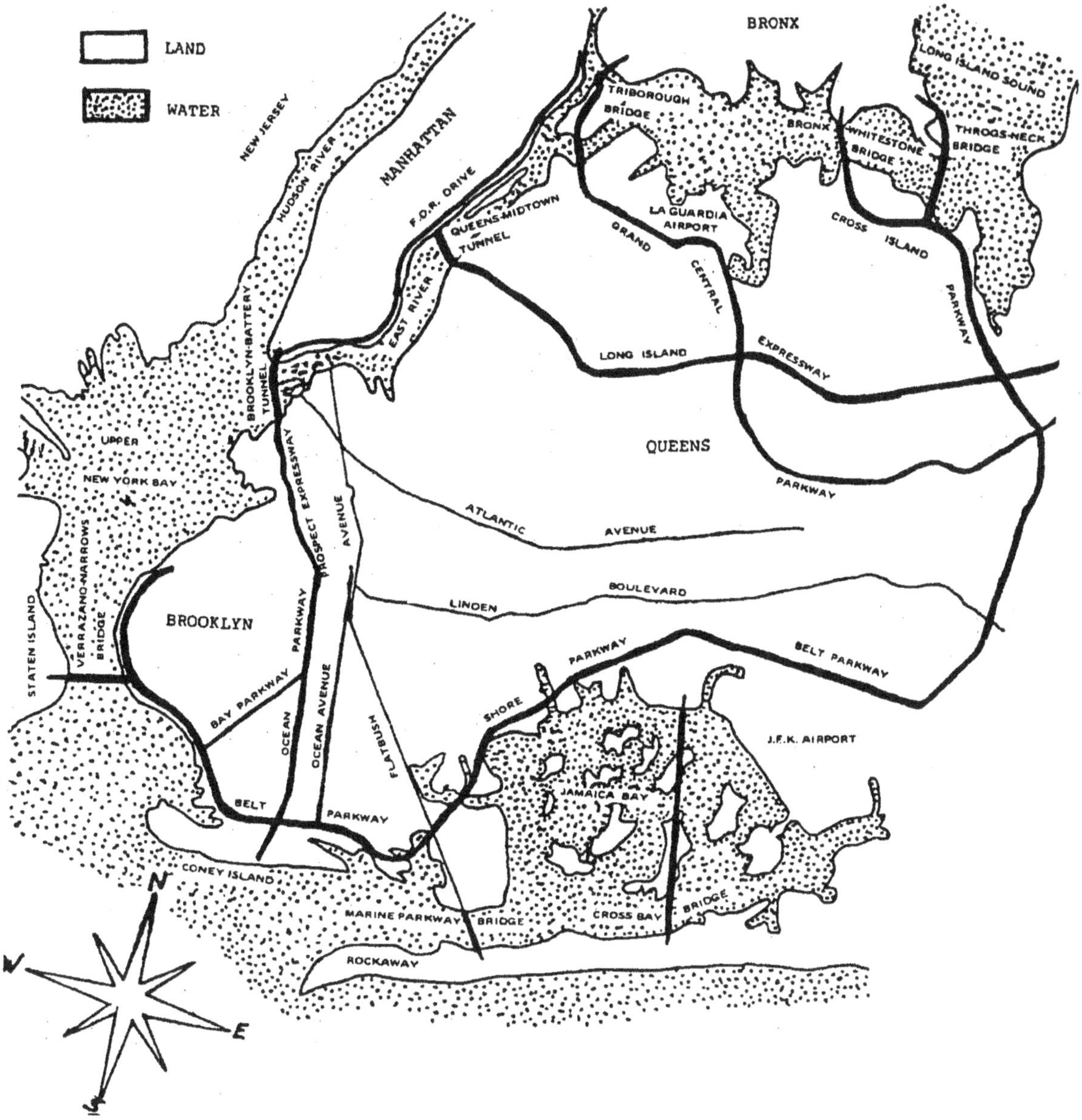

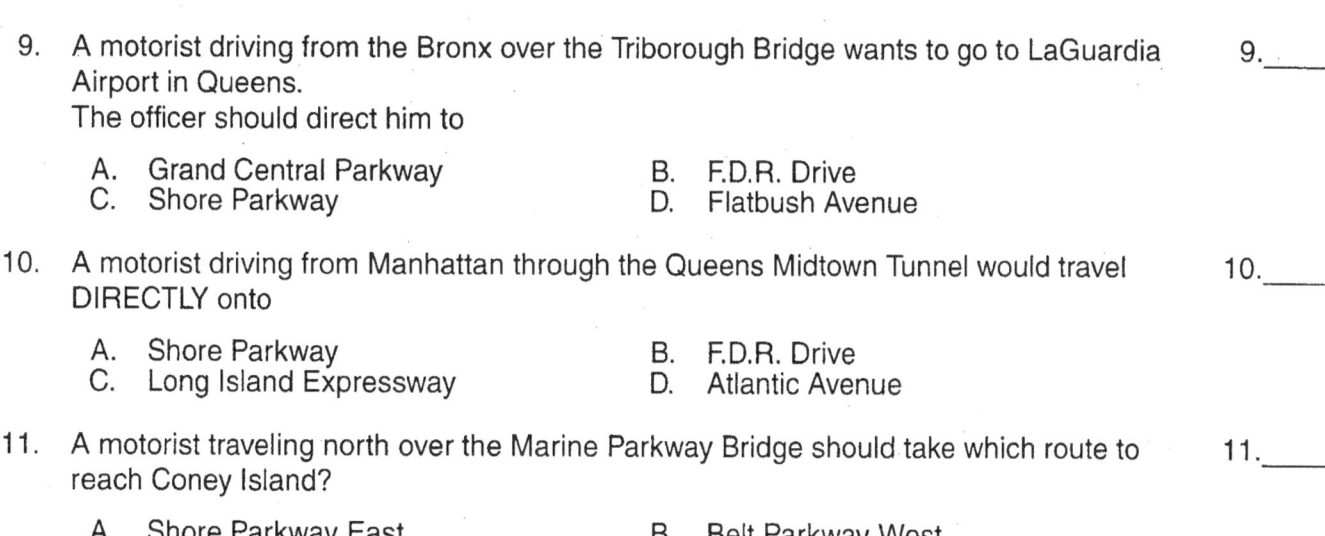

9. A motorist driving from the Bronx over the Triborough Bridge wants to go to LaGuardia Airport in Queens.
   The officer should direct him to

   A. Grand Central Parkway
   B. F.D.R. Drive
   C. Shore Parkway
   D. Flatbush Avenue

10. A motorist driving from Manhattan through the Queens Midtown Tunnel would travel DIRECTLY onto

    A. Shore Parkway
    B. F.D.R. Drive
    C. Long Island Expressway
    D. Atlantic Avenue

11. A motorist traveling north over the Marine Parkway Bridge should take which route to reach Coney Island?

    A. Shore Parkway East
    B. Belt Parkway West
    C. Linden Boulevard
    D. Ocean Parkway

12. Which facility does NOT connect the Bronx and Queens?

    A. Triborough Bridge  
    B. Bronx-Whitestone Bridge  
    C. Verrazano-Narrows Bridge  
    D. Throgs-Neck Bridge

13. A motorist driving from Manhattan arrives at the toll booth of the Brooklyn-Battery Tunnel and asks directions to Ocean Parkway.
    To which one of the following routes should the motorist FIRST be directed?

    A. Atlantic Avenue  
    B. Bay Parkway  
    C. Prospect Expressway  
    D. Ocean Avenue

Questions 14-16.

DIRECTIONS: Questions 14 through 16 are to be answered SOLELY on the basis of the following map. The flow of traffic is indicated by the arrows. If there is only one arrow shown, then traffic flows only in the direction indicated by the arrow. If there are two arrows, then traffic flows in both directions. You must follow the flow of traffic.

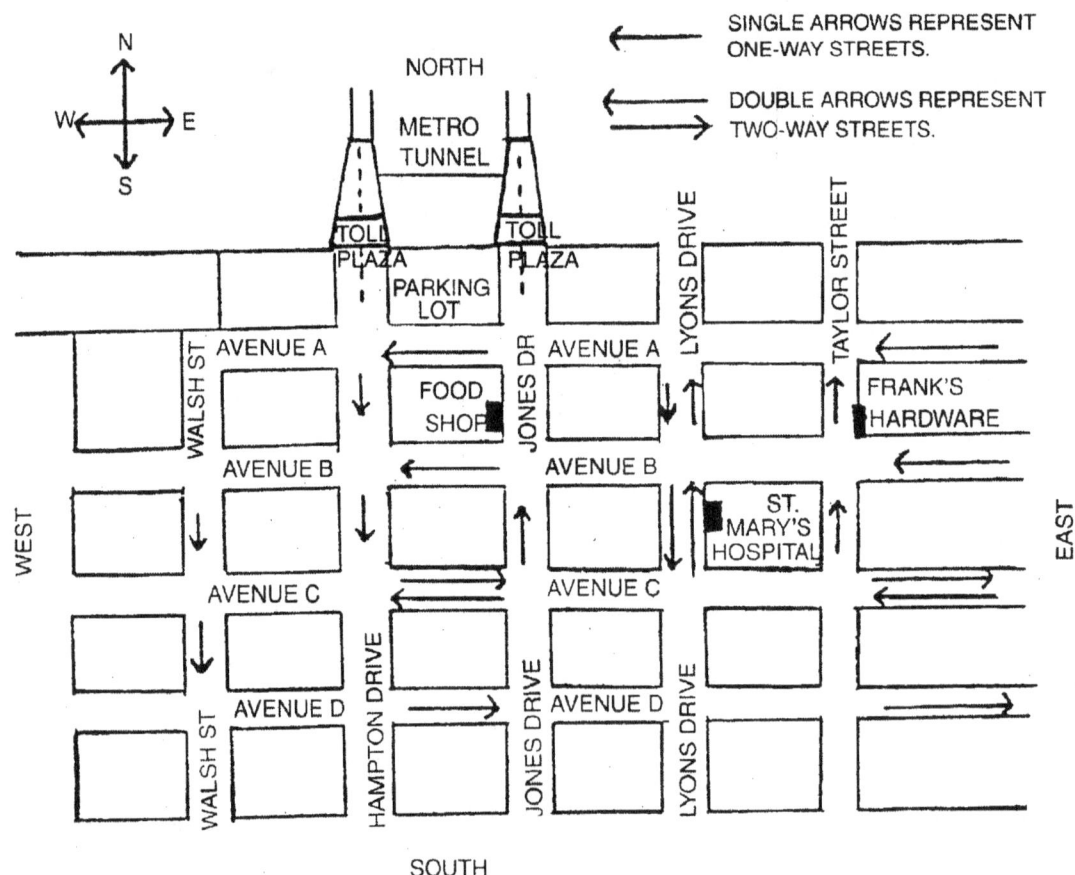

14. A motorist is exiting the Metro Tunnel and approaches the bridge and tunnel officer at the toll plaza. He asks the officer how to get to the food shop on Jones Drive. Which one of the following is the SHORTEST route for the motorist to take, making sure to obey all traffic regulations?
    Travel south on Hampton Drive, then left on _____ on Jones Drive to the food shop.

A. Avenue A, then right  B. Avenue B, then right
C. Avenue D, then left  D. Avenue C, then left

15. A motorist heading south pulls up to a toll booth at the exit of the Metro Tunnel and asks  15.____
Bridge and Tunnel Officer Evans how to get to Frank's Hardware Store on Taylor Street.
Which one of the following is the SHORTEST route for the motorist to take, making sure to obey all traffic regulations?
Travel south on Hampton Drive, then east on

    A. Avenue B to Taylor Street
    B. Avenue D, then north on Taylor Street to Avenue B
    C. Avenue C, then north on Taylor Street to Avenue B
    D. Avenue C, then north on Lyons Drive, then east on Avenue B to Taylor Street

16. A motorist is exiting the Metro Tunnel and approaches the toll plaza. She asks Bridge  16.____
and Tunnel Officer Owens for directions to St. Mary's Hospital.
Which one of the following is the SHORTEST route for the motorist to take, making sure to obey all traffic regulations?
Travel south on Hampton Drive, then _____ on Lyons Drive to St. Mary's Hospital.

    A. left on Avenue D, then left
    B. right on Avenue A, then left on Walsh Street, then left on Avenue D, then left
    C. left on Avenue C, then left
    D. left on Avenue B, then right

Questions 17-18.

DIRECTIONS: Questions 17 and 18 are to be answered SOLELY on the basis of the map which appears on the following page. The flow of traffic is indicated by the arrows. If there is only one arrow shown, then traffic flows only in the direction indicated by the arrow. If there are two arrows shown, then traffic flows in both directions. You must follow the flow of traffic.

8 (#1)

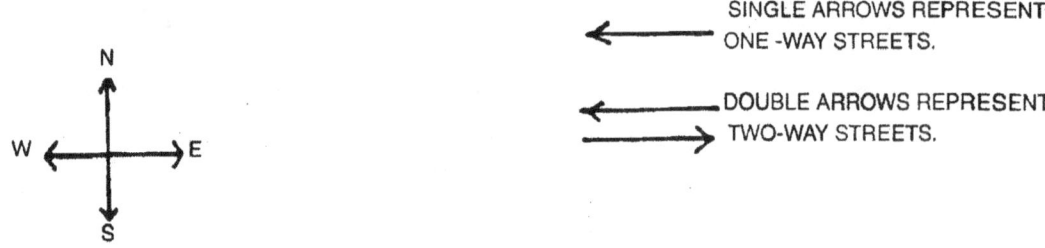

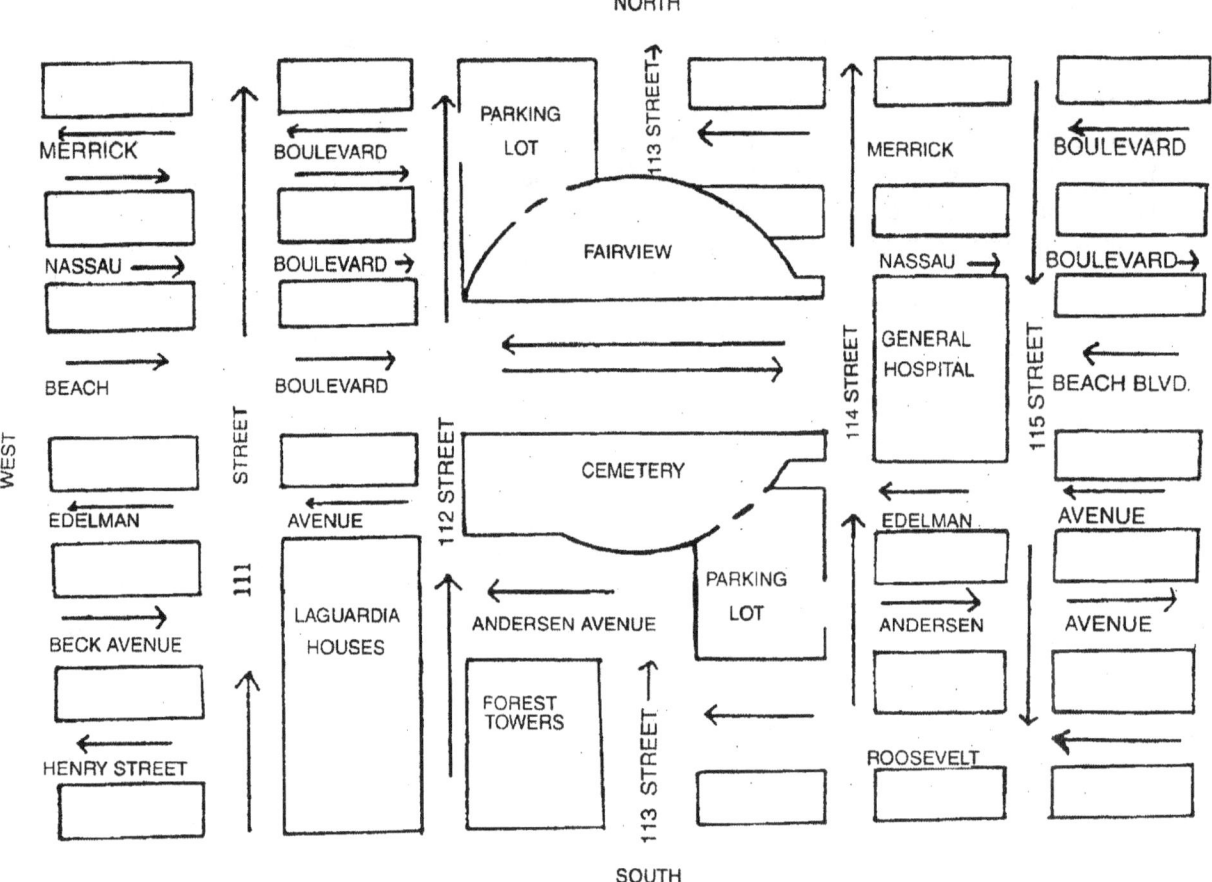

17. Police Officers Glenn and Albertson are on 111th Street at Henry Street when they are dispatched to a past robbery at Beach Boulevard and 115th Street.
Which one of the following is the SHORTEST route for the officers to follow in their patrol car, making sure to obey all traffic regulations?
Travel north on 111th Street, then east on _____ south on 115th Street.

A. Edelman Avenue, then north on 112th Street, then east on Beach Boulevard, then north on 114th Street, then east on Nassau Boulevard, then one block
B. Beach Boulevard, then north on 114th Street, then east on Nassau Boulevard, then one block
C. Merrick Boulevard, then two blocks
D. Nassau Boulevard, then south on 112th Street, then east on Beach Boulevard, then north on 114th Street, then east on Nassau Boulevard, then one block

18. Later in their tour, Officers Glenn and Albertson are driving on 114th Street. If they make a left turn to enter the parking lot at Andersen Avenue, and then make a u-turn, in what direction would they now be headed?

   A. North     B. South     C. East     D. West

Questions 19-20.

DIRECTIONS: Questions 19 and 20 are to be answered SOLELY on the basis of the following map. The flow of traffic is indicated by the arrows. If there is only one arrow shown, then traffic flows only in the direction indicated by the arrow. If there are two arrows shown, then traffic flows in both directions. You must follow the flow of traffic.

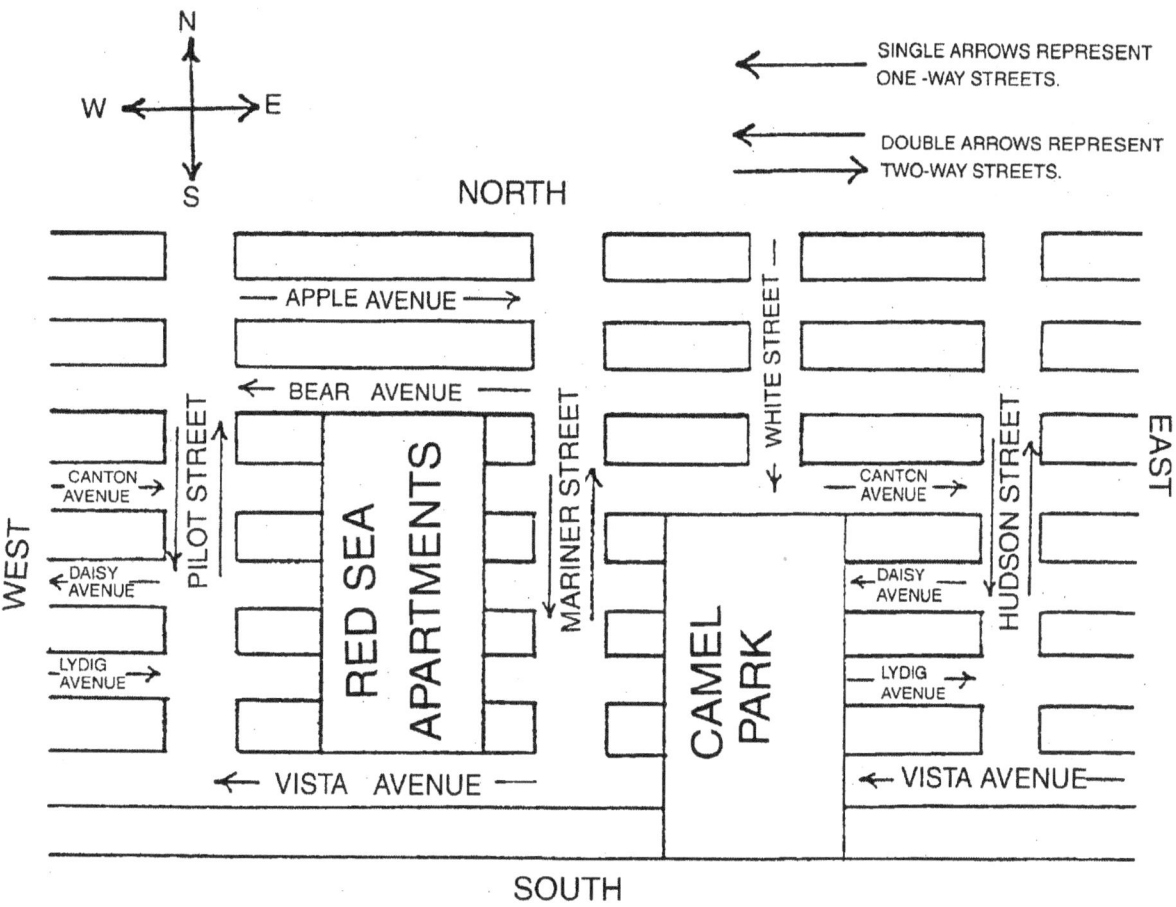

19. You are located at Apple Avenue and White Street. You receive a call to respond to the corner of Lydig Avenue and Pilot Street.
Which one of the following is the MOST direct route for you to take in your patrol car, making sure to obey all traffic regulations?
Travel _____ on Pilot Street.

   A. two blocks south on White Street, then one block east on Canton Avenue, then one block north on Hudson Street, then three blocks west on Bear Avenue, then three blocks south

   B. one block south on White Street, then two blocks west on Bear Avenue, then three blocks south

C. two blocks west on Apple Avenue, then four blocks south
D. two blocks south on White Street, then one block west on Canton Avenue, then three blocks south on Mariner Street, then one block west on Vista Avenue, then one block north

20. You are located at Canton Avenue and Pilot Street. You receive a call of a crime in progress at the intersection of Canton Avenue and Hudson Street.
Which one of the following is the MOST direct route for you to take in your patrol car, making sure to obey all traffic regulations?
Travel

20._____

A. two blocks north on Pilot Street, then two blocks east on Apple Avenue, then one block south on White Street, then one block east on Bear Avenue, then one block south on Hudson Street
B. three blocks south on Pilot Street, then travel one block east on Vista Avenue, then travel three blocks north on Mariner Street, then travel two blocks east on Canton Avenue
C. one block north on Pilot Street, then travel three blocks east on Bear Avenue, then travel one block south on Hudson Street
D. two blocks north on Pilot Street, then travel three blocks east on Apple Avenue, then travel two blocks south on Hudson Street

## KEY (CORRECT ANSWERS)

| | | | |
|---|---|---|---|
| 1. | B | 11. | B/D |
| 2. | D | 12. | C |
| 3. | B | 13. | C |
| 4. | C | 14. | D |
| 5. | A | 15. | C |
| 6. | D | 16. | C |
| 7. | A | 17. | B |
| 8. | B | 18. | C |
| 9. | A | 19. | B |
| 10. | C | 20. | D |

# EXAMINATION SECTION
## TEST 1

DIRECTIONS: Each question or incomplete statement is followed by several suggested answers or completions. Select the one that BEST answers the question or completes the statement. *PRINT THE LETTER OF THE CORRECT ANSWER IN THE SPACE AT THE RIGHT.*

Questions 1-4.

DIRECTIONS: Questions 1 through 4 are to be answered on the basis of the information provided in the paragraph below.

*Rodent control must be planned carefully in order to insure its success. This means that more knowledge is needed about the habits and favorite breeding places of Domestic Rats, than any other kind. A favorite breeding place for Domestic Rats is known to be in old or badly constructed buildings. Rats find these buildings very comfortable for making nests. However, the only way to gain this kind of detailed knowledge about rats is through careful study.*

1. According to the above paragraph, rats find comfortable nesting places  1.____
   - A. in old buildings
   - B. in pipes
   - C. on roofs
   - D. in sewers

2. The paragraph states that the BEST way to learn all about the favorite nesting places of rats is by  2.____
   - A. asking people
   - B. careful study
   - C. using traps
   - D. watching ratholes

3. According to the paragraph, in order to insure the success of rodent control, it is necessary to  3.____
   - A. design better bait
   - B. give out more information
   - C. plan carefully
   - D. use pesticides

4. The paragraph states that the MOST important rats to study are _____ rats.  4.____
   - A. African
   - B. Asian
   - C. Domestic
   - D. European

Questions 5-8.

DIRECTIONS: Questions 5 through 8 are to be answered on the basis of the following paragraph.

*A few people who live in old tenements have the bad habit of throwing garbage out of their windows, especially if there is an empty lot near their building. Sometimes the garbage is food, sometimes the garbage is half-empty soda cans. Sometimes the garbage is a little bit of both mixed together. These people just don't care about keeping the lot clean.*

5. The paragraph states that throwing garbage out of windows is a

   A. bad habit
   B. dangerous thing to do
   C. good thing to do
   D. good way to feed rats

6. According to the paragraph, an empty lot next to an old tenement is sometimes used as a place to

   A. hold local gang meetings
   B. play ball
   C. throw garbage
   D. walk dogs

7. According to the paragraph, which of the following throw garbage out of their windows?

   A. Nobody
   B. Everybody
   C. Most people
   D. Some people

8. According to the paragraph, the kinds of garbage thrown out of windows are

   A. candy and cigarette butts
   B. food and half-empty soda cans
   C. fruit and vegetables
   D. rice and bread

Questions 9-12.

DIRECTIONS: Questions 9 through 12 are to be answered on the basis of the following paragraph.

*The game that is recognised all over the world as an all-American game is the game of baseball. As a matter of fact, baseball heroes like Joe DiMaggio, Willie Mays, and Babe Ruth, were as famous in their day as movie stars Robert Redford, Paul Newman, and Clint Eastwood are now. All these men have had the experience of being mobbed by fans whenever they put in an appearance anywhere in the world. Such unusual popularity makes it possible for stars like these to earn at least as much money off the job as on the job. It didn't take manufacturers and advertising men long to discover that their sales of shaving lotion, for instance, increased when they got famous stars to advertise their product for them on radio and television.*

9. According to the paragraph, baseball is known everywhere as a(n) _____ game.

   A. all-American
   B. fast
   C. unusual
   D. tough

10. According to the paragraph, being so well known means that it is possible for people like Willie Mays and Babe Ruth to

    A. ask for anything and get it
    B. make as much money off the job as on it
    C. travel anywhere free of charge
    D. watch any game free of charge

11. According to the paragraph, which of the following are known all over the world?

    A. Baseball heroes
    B. Advertising men
    C. Manufacturers
    D. Basketball heroes

12. According to the paragraph, it is possible to sell much more shaving lotion on television and radio if   12._____

    A. the commercials are in color instead of black and white
    B. you can get a prize with each bottle of shaving lotion
    C. the shaving lotion makes you smell nicer than usual
    D. the shaving lotion is advertised by famous stars

Questions 13-16.

DIRECTIONS: Questions 13 through 16 are to be answered on the basis of the following paragraph.

*People are very suspicious of all strangers who knock at their door. For this reason, every pest control aide, whether man or woman, must carry an identification card at all times on the job. These cards are issued by the agency the aide works for. The aide's picture is on the card. The aide's name is typed in, and the aide's signature is written on the line below. The name, address, and telephone number of the agency issuing the card is also printed on it. Once the aide shows this ID card to prove his or her identity, the tenant's time should not be taken up with small talk. The tenant should be told briefly what pest control means. The aide should be polite and ready to answer any questions the tenant may have on the subject. Then, the aide should thank the tenant for listening and say goodbye.*

13. According to the above paragraph, when she visits tenants, the one item a pest control aide must ALWAYS carry with her is a(n)   13._____

    A. badge                B. driver's license
    C. identification card  D. watch

14. According to the paragraph, a pest control aide is supposed to talk to each tenant he visits   14._____

    A. at length about the agency
    B. briefly about pest control
    C. at length about family matters
    D. briefly about social security

15. According to the paragraph, the item that does NOT appear on an ID card is the   15._____

    A. address of the agency
    B. name of the agency
    C. signature of the aide
    D. social security number of the aide

16. According to the paragraph, a pest control aide carries an identification card because he must   16._____

    A. prove to tenants who he is
    B. provide the tenants with the agency's address
    C. provide the tenant with the agency's telephone number
    D. save the tenant's time

Questions 17-20.

DIRECTIONS: Questions 17 through 20 are to be answered on the basis of the following paragraph.

*Very early on a summer's morning, the nicest thing to look at is a beach, before the swimmers arrive. Usually all the litter has been picked up from the sand by the Park Department clean-up crew. Everything is quiet. All you can hear are the waves breaking, and the sea gulls calling to each other. The beach opens to the public at 10 A.M. Long before that time, however, long lines of eager men, women, and children have driven up to the entrance. They form long lines that wind around the beach waiting for the signal to move.*

17. According to the paragraph, before 10 A.M., long lines are formed that are made up of     17.____

    A. cars
    B. clean-up crews
    C. men, women, and children
    D. Park Department trucks

18. The season referred to in the above paragraph is     18.____

    A. fall     B. summer     C. winter     D. spring

19. The place the paragraph is describing is a     19.____

    A. beach
    B. park
    C. golf course
    D. tennis court

20. According to the paragraph, one of the things you notice early in the morning is that     20.____

    A. radios are playing
    B. swimmers are there
    C. the sand is dirty
    D. the litter is gone

Questions 21-30.

DIRECTIONS: In Questions 21 through 30, select the answer which means MOST NEARLY the SAME as the capitalized word in the sentence.

21. He received a large REWARD.     21.____
    In this sentence, the word REWARD means

    A. capture
    B. recompense
    C. key
    D. praise

22. The aide was asked to TRANSMIT a message. In this sentence, the word TRANSMIT     22.____
    means

    A. change     B. send     C. take     D. type

23. The pest control aide REQUESTED the tenant to call the Health Department.     23.____
    In this sentence, the word REQUESTED means the pest control aide

    A. asked     B. helped     C. informed     D. warned

24. The driver had to RETURN the Health Department's truck. In this sentence, the word     24.____
    RETURN means

    A. borrow     B. fix     C. give back     D. load up

25. The aide discussed the PURPOSE of the visit. In this sentence, the word PURPOSE means

    A. date    B. hour    C. need    D. reason

26. The tenant SUSPECTED the aide who knocked at her door. In this sentence, the word SUSPECTED means

    A. answered    B. called
    C. distrusted    D. welcomed

27. The aide was POSITIVE that the child hit her. In this sentence, the word POSITIVE means

    A. annoyed    B. certain    C. sorry    D. surprised

28. The tenant DECLINED to call the Health Department. In this sentence, the word DECLINED means

    A. agreed    B. decided    C. refused    D. wanted

29. The aide ARRIVED on time.
    In this sentence, the word ARRIVED means

    A. awoke    B. came    C. left    D. delayed

30. The salesman had to DELIVER books to each person he visited.
    In this sentence, the word DELIVER means

    A. give    B. lend    C. mail    D. sell

## KEY (CORRECT ANSWERS)

| | | |
|---|---|---|
| 1. A | 11. A | 21. B |
| 2. B | 12. D | 22. B |
| 3. C | 13. C | 23. A |
| 4. C | 14. B | 24. C |
| 5. A | 15. D | 25. D |
| 6. C | 16. A | 26. C |
| 7. D | 17. C | 27. B |
| 8. B | 18. B | 28. C |
| 9. A | 19. A | 29. B |
| 10. B | 20. D | 30. A |

# TEST 2

DIRECTIONS: Each question or incomplete statement is followed by several suggested answers or completions. Select the one that BEST answers the question or completes the statement. *PRINT THE LETTER OF THE CORRECT ANSWER IN THE SPACE AT THE RIGHT.*

Questions 1-10.

DIRECTIONS: In Questions 1 through 10, pick the word that means MOST NEARLY the OPPOSITE of the capitalize word in the sentence.

1. It is possible to CONSTRUCT a rat-proof home. The opposite of CONSTRUCT is     1.____
   A. build     B. erect     C. plant     D. wreck

2. The pest control aide had to REPAIR the flat tire. The opposite of the word REPAIR is     2.____
   A. destroy     B. fix     C. mend     D. patch

3. The pest control aide tried to SHOUT the answer. The opposite of the word SHOUT is     3.____
   A. scream     B. shriek     C. whisper     D. yell

4. Daily VISITS are the best.     4.____
   The opposite of the word VISITS is
   A. absences     B. exercises     C. lessons     D. trials

5. It is important to ARRIVE early in the morning. The opposite of the word ARRIVE is     5.____
   A. climb     B. descend     C. enter     D. leave

6. Jorge is a group LEADER.     6.____
   The opposite of the word LEADER is
   A. boss     B. chief     C. follower     D. overseer

7. The EXTERIOR of the house needs painting.     7.____
   The opposite of the word EXTERIOR is
   A. inside     B. outdoors     C. outside     D. surface

8. He CONCEDED the victory.     8.____
   The opposite of the word CONCEDED is
   A. admitted     B. denied     C. granted     D. reported

9. He watched the team BEGIN.     9.____
   The opposite of the word BEGIN is
   A. end     B. fail     C. gather     D. win

10. Your handwriting is ILLEGIBLE.     10.____
    The opposite of the word ILLEGIBLE is
    A. clear     B. confused     C. jumbled     D. unclear

Questions 11-15.

DIRECTIONS: Questions 11 through 15 are to be answered by following the instructions given in each question. Note that 5 possible answers have been given for these questions ONLY. Therefore, for these questions, your choice may be A, B, C, D, or E.

11. Add:
    $12\frac{1}{2}$
    $2\frac{1}{4}$
    $3\frac{1}{4}$

    The CORRECT answer is

    A. 17   B. 174   C. 174   D. 17 3/4   E. 18

12. Subtract: 150
    -80

    The CORRECT answer is

    A. 70   B. 80   C. 130   D. 150   E. 230

13. After cleaning up some lots in the East Bronx, five cleanup crews loaded the following amounts of garbage on trucks:
    Crew No. 1 loaded 2 1/4 tons
    Crew No. 2 loaded 3 tons
    Crew No. 3 loaded 1 1/4 tons
    Crew No. 4 loaded 2 1/4 tons
    Crew No. 5 loaded 1/2 ton
    The TOTAL number of tons of garbage loaded was

    A. 8   B. 8 1/4   C. 8 3/4   D. 9   E. 9 1/4

14. Subtract: 17 3/4
    - 7 1/4

    The CORRECT answer is

    A. 7 1/2   B. 10 1/2   C. 14 1/4   D. 17 3/4   E. 25

15. Yesterday, Tom and Bill each received 10 leaflets about rat control. Each supermarket in the neighborhood was supposed to receive one of these leaflets. When the day was over, Tom had 8 leaflets left. Bill had no leaflets left. How many supermarkets got leaflets yesterday?

    A. 8   B. 10   C. 12   D. 18   E. 20

Questions 16-20.

DIRECTIONS: Questions 16 through 20 are to be answered ONLY on the basis of the information in the following statement and chart, DAILY WORK REPORT FORM (Chart A).

*Assume that you are a member of the Pest Control Truck Crew Number 1. Julio Rivera is your Crew Chief. The crew is supposed to report to work at nine o'clock in the morning, Since you are the first to show up, at ten minutes before nine, on 5/24 Rivera asks you to help him out by filling in the Daily Work Report Form for him. Driver Hal Williams shows up at nine, and Driver Rick Smith shows up ten minutes after Williams.*

DAILY WORK REPORT FORM (Chart A)

| Block #1 Crew No. | Block #2 Date | |
|---|---|---|
| Block #3 TRUCKS IN USE Truck # # # # # # # # # | Block #4 DRIVER'S NAME | Block #5 TIME OF ARRIVAL A.M.          P.M. |
| Block #6 TRUCKS OUT OF ORDER # # # # # | Block #7 ADDRESS OF CLEAN-UP SITE No._____ Street_____ | Block #8 Borough Block #9 Signature of Crew Chief |

16. According to the above statement, the entry that belongs in Block #9 is

    A. Julio Rivera   B. June Stevens
    C. Jim Watson    D. Hal Williams

17. According to the above statement, the entry that should be made in Block #2 is

    A. 9:00 A.M.   B. 9:10 P.M.   C. 5/24   D. 7/24

18. The names of Hal Williams and Rick Smith should appear in Block #

    A. 4   B. 6   C. 7   D. 9

19. Rick Smith's time of arrival should be entered in Block #5 as _____ A.M.   19._____

    A. 8:50   B. 8:55   C. 9:00   D. 9:10

20. According to the statement, the entry that should be made in Block #1 is   20._____

    A. zero   B. one   C. 5/24   D. 6/24

Questions 21-23.

DIRECTIONS: Questions 21 through 23 are to be answered on the basis of the statement shown below. Use DAILY WORK REPORT FORM (Chart A) on Page 3 as a guide.

*Pete Marberg showed up at a quarter after nine, in the morning, but his truck, No. 22632441, was in the garage for repairs. Steve Marino showed up a half hour after Pete. He was assigned truck No. 6342003, which was in working order.*

21. According to the above statement, truck No. 22632441 should be entered in Block #   21._____

    A. 3   B. 4   C. 6   D. 8

22. According to the above statement, Steve Marino showed up at   22._____

    A. 9:00 A.M.   B. 9:15 A.M.   C. 9:30 P.M.   D. 9:45 A.M.

23. According to the above statement, Steve Marino's truck number belongs in Block #3. The number entered there should be   23._____

    A. 22632441   B. 6342003   C. 6432003   D. 26232441

Questions 24-30.

DIRECTIONS: Questions 24 through 30 are to be answered ONLY on basis of the information in the statements above ea question and the following chart, DAILY GARBAGE COLLECTION REPORT (Chart B).

| DAILY GARBAGE COLLECTION REPORT C Chart B) | | | | |
|---|---|---|---|---|
| Block #1 | Block #2 | Block #3 | Block #4 | Block #5 |
| No. of Trucks Used For Collection | Address of Garbage Pick-Up | Amount of Garbage Collected | Amount of Garbage Unloaded | Hours During Which Garbage Was Unloaded |
| #456 | 45 Southwest | 1/2 ton | 1/2 ton | From 7 AM  To 8 AM |
| TOTALS _____ | | Block #6 otal Amount of Garbage Collected By All Trucks | Block #7 Total Amount of Garbage Unloaded By All Trucks | Block #8 Total Amount of Time Spent Unloading Of All Trucks |
| | | | | |

24. Truck # 2437752 started unloading garbage at ten o'clock Monday morning and finished unloading its garbage that afternoon. The clock looked like this when the job was done.
The time entries that should be recorded in Block #5 are
   A. 10 A.M. and 12:15 P.M.
   B. 10 P.M. and 12:30 A.M.
   C. 10 P.M. and 12:00 A.M.
   D. 10 A.M. and 3:00 P.M.

24.____

25. Truck # 8967432 had to pick up a load of garbage from 911 South Avenue. It took the crew until 11:00 A.M. to load the garbage.
According to this statement, the item 911 South Avenue should be entered in Block #

   A. 1     B. 2     C. 3     D. 4

25.____

26. On Tuesday, truck # 124356 unloaded 4 ton of garbage, truck # 2437752 unloaded J ton of garbage, and truck # 435126 unloaded 1/2 ton of garbage.
The TOTAL amount of garbage unloaded by the three trucks on Tuesday should be entered in Block #

   A. 3     B. 4     C. 5     D. 8

26.____

27. On Wednesday, it took truck # 4050607 from 2 P.M. to 6 P.M. to unload 1 ton of garbage. It took truck # 7040650 from 1 P.M. to 2 P.M. to unload 1/4 ton of garbage. These were the only trucks working that day.
The TOTAL amount of time it took for both trucks to unload garbage was _____ hours.

   A. 5     B. 6     C. 7     D. 8

27.____

28. The amount of garbage collected by one truck should be entered in the DAILY GARBAGE COLLECTION REPORT FORM in Block #

   A. 3     B. 6     C. 7     D. 8

28.____

29. Truck # 557799010 reported to 1020 Hudson River Alley to pick up garbage from an empty lot.
This information should be entered in the DAILY GARBAGE COLLECTION REPORT FORM in Block # _____ and Block # _____ .

   A. 1; 4     B. 2; 5     C. 1; 2     D. 2; 3

29.____

30. It took the Pest Control Truck crew from 8 in the morning to 12 noon to unload the garbage it collected the night before.
    This information should be entered in the DAILY GARBAGE COLLECTION REPORT FORM under Block #
    
    A. 4   B. 5   C. 6   D. 7

30.____

---

# KEY (CORRECT ANSWERS)

| | | |
|---|---|---|
| 1. D | 11. E | 21. C |
| 2. A | 12. A | 22. D |
| 3. C | 13. E | 23. B |
| 4. A | 14. B | 24. D |
| 5. D | 15. C | 25. B |
| 6. C | 16. A | 26. B |
| 7. A | 17. C | 27. A |
| 8. B | 18. A | 28. A |
| 9. A | 19. D | 29. C |
| 10. A | 20. B | 30. B |

---

# READING COMPREHENSION
## UNDERSTANDING AND INTERPRETING WRITTEN MATERIAL
# EXAMINATION SECTION
# TEST 1

DIRECTIONS: Each question consists of a statement. You are to indicate whether the statement is TRUE (T) or FALSE (F). *PRINT THE LETTER OF THE CORRECT ANSWER IN THE SPACE AT THE RIGHT.*

Questions 1-10.

DIRECTIONS: Questions 1 through 10 are based on the following passage.

When a summons is used in lieu of an arrest for an unlawful act, the Inspector should first make certain of the offender's identity. The summonses are always made returnable to the local district city Magistrates' Court having jurisdiction in the area in which the offense is committed. Inspectors issuing such summons should allow at least a twenty-four hour period to elapse between the time of service and the time for arraignment. At the completion of each Inspector's tour, a card is submitted to the Division Office, describing in detail the violator, his address, the violation, place of occurrence, court, and returnable date.

The summons (or arrest) cards are carefully checked against the Premises File and also against an Alphabetical File for previous offenders; and when previous records are disclosed, the office is notified of the offender's past record in order that such information may be passed along to the city Magistrate presiding at the trial.

1. A summons cannot be issued in place of an arrest.  1.____

2. Before a summons is issued, an inspector should make sure of the identity of the offender.  2.____

3. Summonses are always returnable to the local district city Magistrates' Court having jurisdiction over the area in which the offense was committed.  3.____

4. Inspectors should allow at least 24 days to elapse between time of service and time for arraignment.  4.____

5. A card is submitted after each tour by an Inspector which, among other things, describes the violator, his address, and the violation.  5.____

6. The card submitted should also include the place of occurrence, the court, and the returnable date.  6.____

7. The summons cards are checked against a file for previous offenders.  7.____

8. When a previous record is disclosed, it is filed in the Magistrates' Court.  8.____

9. The officer is notified of a previous record so that the presiding magistrate can be aware of the situation at the trial.  9.____

10. Summonses are usually issued to men already under arrest.  10.____

Questions 11-25.

DIRECTIONS: Questions 11 through 25 are based on the statements given below. Your answers to these questions must be based ONLY on the information given in this passage and not on any other information you may have.

Formerly, all the records on material were kept on a volume basis (cubic yards), but a few years ago this was changed to the more accurate weight basis. Since we do not have scales at all locations, approximate weights have been set for different types of vehicles with allowance being made for the difference between summer and winter material. Sanitation men must be familiar with these established weights since they are used daily in converting yardage load figures to conform to the present requirements of our statistics. In addition, at the incinerators a maximum weight for various vehicles is set as they indicate an overload of non-combustible material such as ashes.

Certain city agencies and recognized charitable organizations are permitted to use dumping facilities without cost, but only if they are on our approved list and their own vehicles are used. Examples of such organizations are the Salvation Army and Catholic Charities. City agencies, such as the Borough Public Works and the Park Department, likewise are accorded free dumping privileges, but they are subject to our rules in regard to non-combustible materials. Government and state agencies are required to pay for dumping privileges the same as anyone else.

The officer at any of our locations has no discretion in regard to permitting private concerns the privilege of dumping without paying therefor and without conforming to our regulations.

On very rare occasions, a concern such as a bank may be required to witness the destruction by burning of certain checks or records. When this occurs, arrangements have to be made by the concern through the main office, and even then the officer at the location must not permit them to dispose of the material until after calling the main office for permission. The procedure applies to each and every load so disposited, and in all cases an entry of the incident must be made in the log.

11. Records kept on a volume basis are more accurate than weight records.  11.____

12. The Department of Sanitation has scales at all disposal locations.  12.____

13. Because of the shortage of time, volume records are kept at some locations.  13.____

14. Allowances are made in the approximate weights set for different types of vehicles according to the seasons.  14.____

15. A sanitation man can easily convert yardage load figures to weight figures with the knowledge of the established weight for different type vehicles.  15.____

16. A maximum weight is set for various vehicles at incinerators since greater amounts indicate an overload of noncombustible material.  16.____

17. Any charitable agency may have the Department of Sanitation take their refuse to a city dump. 17._____

18. The Salvation Army and similar approved charitable organizations may dump freely at a city dump if they use their own truck. 18._____

19. City agencies have free dumping privileges for combustible materials. 19._____

20. Government and state agencies are exempt from fees for dumping privileges. 20._____

21. An officer at a Department of Sanitation location may, in some cases, grant a private concern special privileges of dumping without payment and without conforming to Department of Sanitation regulations. 21._____

22. Banks or similar concerns may arrange to have witnesses present at the burning of checks or records. 22._____

23. A bank wishing to make arrangements to burn records must first contact the nearest incinerator plant. 23._____

24. Each load which requires a witness must be arranged for independently. 24._____

25. Where arrangements are made to burn records, an entry of the incident must be made in the log. 25._____

## KEY (CORRECT ANSWERS)

1. F
2. T
3. T
4. F
5. T

6. T
7. T
8. F
9. T
10. F

11. F
12. F
13. F
14. T
15. T

16. T
17. F
18. T
19. T
20. F

21. F
22. T
23. F
24. T
25. T

# TEST 2

DIRECTIONS: Each question consists of a statement. You are to indicate whether the statement is TRUE (T) or FALSE (F). *PRINT THE LETTER OF THE CORRECT ANSWER IN THE SPACE AT THE RIGHT.*

Questions 1-20.

DIRECTIONS: Questions 1 through 20 are to be answered according to the information given in the paragraphs below.

The responsibility of the Bureau of Street Cleaning and Waste Collection of the Department of Sanitation is to render sanitary service for approximately 7,500,000 resident taxpayers and 2,500,000 transients who visit the city daily from neighboring states.

Sanitary service includes the collection and removal of refuse, sweeping, cleaning, washing and sanding of only those streets under Department jurisdiction, removal of dead animals, and removal of snow and ice during the winter season.

For the perforance of these functions, the Bureau maintains an office of The Assistant to Commissioner, a city office, seven borough offices, sixty-one district offices and fifty-seven garages, through which all orders, notices and directives are transmitted, guiding the work of the field forces in the performance of their various assignments.

To maintain close supervision as a medium for obtaining the utmost in operating efficiency, the Bureau's sixty-one districts are subdivided into two hundred and forty-eight sections, an average of approximately four sections per district.

Each district is staffed with a superintendent, foremen, assistant foreman, and other personnel and equipment as is required for the proper performance of work. Districts vary in population from 10,500 to 350,000 persons, a square area ranging from 6/10 mile to 21 miles.

The work is regulated on the basis of established schedules and procedures, variations being introduced at frequent intervals as a means of promoting greater efficiency. Although each district operates as a distinct unit and in accordance with its particular requirements, the scheme of operating is so arranged as to coordinate with the work of adjoining districts. This arrangement follows throughout the various boroughs and provides for the servicing of the entire city.

1. Sanitation districts are subdivided into sections.  1.___
2. There is the same number of borough offices as there are boroughs.  2.___
3. There is a garage attached to each district.  3.___
4. There are approximately four sections to each district.  4.___
5. Each district is headed by a foreman.  5.___
6. The department renders service to approximately 10,000,000 persons daily.  6.___

7. One-third of the city's daily population is composed of transients.  7.____

8. Sanitary service does not include the removal of dead animals.  8.____

9. The department sweeps and cleans all streets in the city.  9.____

10. Directives to the field forces are transmitted through the district offices.  10.____

11. No district is less than 4 mile square.  11.____

12. No district is more than 21 miles wide.  12.____

13. The largest population of any district is 350,000 people.  13.____

14. The smallest districts have a population of at least 10,500 people.  14.____

15. There is no variation in schedules and procedures.  15.____

16. Snow removal is not handled by the Bureau of Street Cleaning and Waste Collection.  16.____

17. Each district operates as a distinct unit.  17.____

18. If each section has one assistant foreman, there must be at least 248 assistant foremen in the bureau.  18.____

19. The number of superintendents in this bureau is at least 61.  19.____

20. Each district coordinates its operations with those of adjoining districts.  20.____

Questions 21-30.

DIRECTIONS: Questions 21 through 30 are to answered according to the information given in the paragraphs below.

About 800 supervisors of all grades have been indoctrinated in corrective methods for unsafe practices and conditions. These instructions help to prevent accidental injuries to the men in their charge. New employees, as a part of their instruction at the Training Center, are given an outline of the safety work and the accident prevention operations of the department by an officer of this division.

An essential part of this work is the reporting of all personal injuries involving loss of time of one or more working days. As an indication of the success of this work, it can be shown that during 2009 there was a decrease under 2008 of 14.2% in the number of employee injuries causing loss of one day or more?

21. There are 900 supervisors who help prevent accidental injuries to the men in their charge.  21.____

22. The supervisors have been taught how to correct unsafe practices and conditions.  22.____

23. The instructions in safety are of no help in preventing accidents.  23.____

24. New employees are given safety instructions at the Training Center. 24.____

25. It is necessary to report only injuries involving loss of more than five days of working time. 25.____

26. It is necessary to report only injuries involving loss of property. 26.____

27. Reporting any injuries is not essential to constructive safety work. 27.____

28. The success of this accident prevention work can be shown by the decrease in employee injuries. 28.____

29. In 2008 there were 14.2% less employee injuries than in 2009. 29.____

30. The injuries referred to are those causing the loss of one day or more. 30.____

## KEY (CORRECT ANSWERS)

| | | | | | |
|---|---|---|---|---|---|
| 1. | T | 11. | T | 21. | F |
| 2. | F | 12. | T | 22. | T |
| 3. | F | 13. | T | 23. | F |
| 4. | T | 14. | T | 24. | T |
| 5. | F | 15. | F | 25. | F |
| 6. | T | 16. | F | 26. | F |
| 7. | F | 17. | T | 27. | F |
| 8. | F | 18. | T | 28. | T |
| 9. | F | 19. | T | 29. | F |
| 10. | T | 20. | T | 30. | T |

# TEST 3

DIRECTIONS: Each question consists of a statement. You are to indicate whether the statement is TRUE (T) or FALSE (F). *PRINT THE LETTER OF THE CORRECT ANSWER IN THE SPACE AT THE RIGHT.*

Questions 1-15.

DIRECTIONS: Questions 1 through 15 are to be answered SOLELY on the information given in the statement below.

New York City, the hub of industrial and financial activities and the home of 8,000,000 inhabitants, maintains a foremost position by the attention it gives to the removal of snow and ice from city streets. The importance of this task can be appreciated if we consider the catastrophe that would result if a snowstorm were inadequately combatted: Traffic would be paralyzed; food and fuel shipments hindered; fire trucks, ambulances, and other emergency vehicles seriously impeded; transportation generally hampered. Small wonder, then, that the function of snow removal is clearly mandated to the Department of Sanitation by Paragraph 755 of the City Charter. The department's operational standards, skilled personnel, and special equipment are designed to cope with this seasonal emergency.

To combat a snowstorm effectively from its start, our department uses a variety of equipment. Each phase of the storm calls for the use of special equipment. The beginning of a storm, depending upon its anticipated intensity, usually brings into operation rotary brooms and sand and salt spreaders. As the storm increases, the plow equipment gains in importance. Each following activity, such as sewering, piling, and flushing, calls for a special type of equipment which by its proper and timely use marks the difference between success and failure.

The best conceived plan and the most adequate equipment are useless without the personnel capable of putting the plan into effect.

For that reason, conscientious and skilled employees are chosen and trained as field instructors through whom other employees are taught the effective use and care of equipment.

1. New York City has eight million inhabitants.    1.____
2. New York City's attention to the removal of snow and ice from the streets has no effect on its foremost position.    2.____
3. If snow were not removed after a snowstorm, traffic would be paralyzed.    3.____
4. A snowstorm has little effect on food and fuel shipments.    4.____
5. Snow removal is mandated to the Department of Sanitation by the City Charter.    5.____
6. The department has special equipment designed to cope with this seasonal emergency.    6.____
7. To fight a snowstorm, the City needs little variety of equipment.    7.____

8. During each part of a storm, special equipment is called into use as needed.  8.___

9. The start of a storm brings out rotary brooms and sand and salt spreaders.  9.___

10. If a storm increases, plows are used.  10.___

11. With a good plan and good equipment, one can put the plan into effect without capable personnel.  11.___

12. Conscientious and skilled employees are chosen and trained as field inspectors.  12.___

13. Other employees are taught the effective use of equipment by the field instructors.  13.___

14. The field instructors should not develop their students' skills as operators of snow equipment.  14.___

15. An instructor should impress the student with the need to apply his skill in effectively using equipment to remove snow.  15.___

Questions 16-25.

DIRECTIONS: The following lists some of the equipment required for street operations. A brief description of the use of each article is noted. Questions 16 through 25 should be answered using the information below.

| | |
|---|---|
| Push brooms | Hand sweeping |
| Panscraper | Rough cleaning |
| Can carrier | Conveying cans of street dirt |
| Shovel | Picking up street dirt |
| Hose reel | Convey hose |
| Nozzle | Regulate water flow |
| Pick | For ice conditions |
| Hydrant pump | Pump water from hydrant barrel |
| Red flags and lanterns | Signal of danger |
| Wire baskets | Pedestrians' litter |
| Solar cans | Pedestrians' litter |
| Can shed | Storage of dirt cans |

16. A panscraper is used for fine cleaning.  16.___

17. A hose reel is used to carry hose.  17.___

18. A can carrier is used to carry cans of street dirt.  18.___

19. A push broom is used to sweep curbs mechanically.  19.___

20. A shovel is used to pick up snow.  20.___

21. A hose is used to wash streets.  21.___

22. A pick is used to pick up street dirt.  22.___

23. A nozzle is used to connect hose to a hydrant. 23._____

24. Red flags and lantern are danger signals. 24._____

25. Wire baskets and solar cans are used for the same purpose. 25._____

## KEY (CORRECT ANSWERS)

1. T
2. F
3. T
4. F
5. T

6. T
7. F
8. T
9. T
10. T

11. F
12. T
13. T
14. F
15. T

16. F
17. T
18. T
19. F
20. F

21. T
22. F
23. F
24. T
25. T

# READING COMPREHENSION
## UNDERSTANDING AND INTERPRETING WRITTEN MATERIAL
# EXAMINATION SECTION
# TEST 1

DIRECTIONS: Each question or incomplete statement is followed by several suggested answers or completions. Select the one that BEST answers the question or completes the statement. *PRINT THE LETTER OF THE CORRECT ANSWER IN THE SPACE AT THE RIGHT.*

Questions 1-8.

DIRECTIONS: Questions 1 through 8 are to be answered SOLELY on the basis of the information given in the following passage.

Machine flushing is the process of washing the street and forcibly pushing the street dirt toward the curbs by directing streams of water under pressure onto the surface of the street from a moving vehicle. Flushers have been known to clean as little as 1 1/2 miles and as much as 41 miles of street during a single 8 hour shift. The average for an 8 hour shift, as shown in a survey made of 36 cities, is 22 miles. The rather large variance is due to wide ranges in operating speeds of the flushers.

The number of shifts that are operated varies considerably among cities. Small communities usually are able to do the required cleaning in a single shift. Most of the larger cities, on the other hand, operate two shifts, and New York City has three shifts daily. New York City also has used chlorinated sea water during water shortages.

As in other kinds of cleaning, the work should be done when traffic is lightest. Parked vehicles do not significantly interfere with flushing, although a better job is done when there are but few cars standing at the curbs.

Flushers are particularly effective when the pavements are wet during and after rains. The rain softens the dirt, and the flushing water moves it away more easily. Substantially less water is required when pavements are wet, and the flushers can travel faster without decreasing their effectiveness. However, since the average citizen is not aware of these advantages, care should be exercised lest the impression be given that the city is watering the lawn while it is raining.

Flushers should not be used in freezing weather or when the temperature is near the freezing point. They may cause icy surfaces to form thereby increasing the chances of traffic accidents. Therefore, water should never be used on pavements unless it is certain that it can evaporate or run off before it freezes.

1. Based on the information in the above passage, it is reasonable to assume that the MAIN reason for using water under pressure in machine flushing is to

   A. prevent wasting of water during shortages
   B. move the dirt to the curb
   C. make sure that the street is thoroughly wet
   D. clear the dirt that is at the curb

2. Based on the information in the above passage, a flusher that cleans 72 miles of street during a 16 hour period is operating at a rate _____ average.

   A. well above the
   B. exactly
   C. slightly less than
   D. well below the

3. According to the above passage, if there are a few cars standing at the curb when machine flushing is being done, the cleaning job

   A. can still be done adequately
   B. will be as effective as when there are many cars parked at the curb
   C. will be better than if there are no cars parked at the curb
   D. will be done poorly

4. Based on the information in the above passage, which one of the following is the MOST probable reason why New York City has three shifts daily for machine flushing operations?

   A. There is more personnel available for use in New York City.
   B. New York City has more water available than other cities.
   C. New York City's budget allows more money for flushing operations.
   D. All the necessary cleaning can't be done with fewer shifts.

5. According to the above passage, the flushing of streets during rain may

   A. take longer than street flushing in dry weather
   B. look like a poor practice to the public
   C. decrease the effectiveness of flushing operations
   D. cause a substantial waste of water

6. In the above passage, which of the following is NOT offered as an advantage of flushing streets when they are wet?

   A. Street dirt more pliable
   B. Street dirt easier to move
   C. Flusher can move faster
   D. Fewer pedestrians and traffic

7. As used in the above passage, the phrase *watering the lawn while it is raining* means to imply that the city is

   A. trying to impress the public
   B. not aware of the opinions of the average citizen
   C. giving its lawns too much water
   D. doing something unnecessary

8. According to the above passage, flushers should NOT be used in freezing weather because

   A. the water may freeze inside the flushers
   B. slippery driving conditions may be created
   C. evaporation or run-off of the water from the pavement is likely
   D. flushers can't move on icy surfaces

Questions 9-11.

DIRECTIONS: Questions 9 through 11 are to be answered SOLELY on the basis of the following paragraphs.

### TYPES OF FILL

Any type of mineral earth or rock can be used as road fill, but clay and silt are generally undesirable. They soften when wet, frequently with changes in volume, and may act as a wick to bring ground water to the surface. Humus is avoided, particularly in its pure state, because of lack of bearing strength and excessive water absorption. Topsoil, a mixture of mineral soil and humus, may or may not be permissible, depending on its qualities and its location in the fill.

Sand and loose, clean gravel have excellent bearing power but afford poor traction, are hard to compact, and must be held in by other materials.

The most desirable fills are mixtures of two or more simple types. Varying proportions of clay, silt, sand, gravel, and stones are found in loams, boulder clay, and glacial till. Sand and gravel are most desirable when mixed with enough clay or silt to bind them together.

Light soils with a high percentage of sand or gravel are desirable when work must be done in rainy places or seasons. They absorb and drain off large quantities of water, and do not get slippery easily.

9. According to the above paragraphs, one of the reasons why sand alone is NOT a good material for fill is that sand

   A. is difficult to obtain          B. is hard to compact
   C. has poor bearing power          D. is expensive to purchase

10. According to the above paragraphs, the one of the following soils that is BEST for fills is

    A. clay
    B. humus
    C. gravel
    D. a mixture of sand, gravel, and clay

11. In rainy weather, the BEST type of fill material to work with is one containing a high percentage of

    A. clay                B. silt
    C. gravel              D. humus

Questions 12-15.

DIRECTIONS: Questions 12 through 15 are to be answered SOLELY on the basis of the following paragraph. Each question consists of a statement. You are to indicate

The number of containers picked up per mile is a better index of the labor requirements for the pick-up operation than the number of houses served per mile. The labor time needed to collect refuse over a given distance increases in direct proportion to the number of containers which must be lifted. It has been found that the number of houses serviced per mile is quite adequate as an index of labor requirements in those cities where the garbage and domestic refuse is deposited in a single standard container and the practice is enforced by law, but in such cases the number of houses serviced is equal to the number of containers picked up.

12. The greater the number of containers of refuse which must be lifted within a given distance traveled, the greater the labor time required to collect the refuse over the distance.

13. The number of houses serviced per mile sometimes equals the number of containers picked up per mile by the collector.

14. The number of houses serviced per mile is not an adequate index of the labor requirements for the pick-up operation in any city.

15. In those cities where the practice of depositing garbage and domestic refuse in separate standard containers is enforced by law, the number of houses serviced per mile is a good index of labor requirements.

Questions 16-21.

DIRECTIONS: Questions 16 through 21 are to be answered SOLELY on the basis of the following paragraph. Each question consists of a statement. You are to indicate whether the statement is TRUE (T) or FALSE (F).

Those unplanned and undesirable occurrences which injure people, destroy equipment and materials, interrupt the orderly progress of any activity, or waste time and money are called accidents. Some degree of hazard is associated with every form of activity, and every uncontrolled hazard will in time produce its share of accidents. Accidents do not just happen. They are caused by unsafe conditions or unsafe acts or both. A safety program is an organized effort to eliminate physical hazards and unsafe practices in order to prevent accidents and their resultant injuries. Safety is not something to be thought of only when no other duties are pressing, but must become part of every activity of every day.

16. A happening that is not wanted and not planned and wastes time and money is called an accident.

17. There is no activity that is free of hazard.

18. Hazardous conditions are uncontrollable.

19. An accident will not happen if the physical conditions are safe.

20. A safety program seeks to prevent accidents by getting rid of unsafe practices and physical hazards.

21. Safety is apart from every day activities.

Questions 22-25.

DIRECTIONS: Questions 22 through 25 are to be answered SOLELY on the basis of the following paragraph. Each question consists of a statement. You are to indicate whether the statement is TRUE (T) or FALSE (F).

In a comparison made between collection by means of open-body trucks and collection by means of mechanical packers, it was found that refuse collectors working with mechanical compaction trucks spent approximately seven percent of the pick-up time in waiting. Only two percent of the pick-up time was consumed by collectors in waiting in the case of collection by open-body trucks.

22. In the comparison made, more than one type of truck was used.

23. A mechanical compaction truck travels more slowly than an open-body truck.

24. A comparison indicates that collectors spend a smaller percentage of pick-up time in waiting when they work with open-body trucks than when they work with mechanical compaction trucks.

25. In refuse collection, type of truck used is a factor influencing time spent on one element of the operation.

## KEY (CORRECT ANSWERS)

| | | | |
|---|---|---|---|
| 1. | B | 11. | C |
| 2. | A | 12. | T |
| 3. | A | 13. | T |
| 4. | D | 14. | F |
| 5. | B | 15. | F |
| 6. | D | 16. | T |
| 7. | D | 17. | T |
| 8. | B | 18. | F |
| 9. | B | 19. | F |
| 10. | D | 20. | T |

21. F
22. T
23. F
24. T
25. T

# TEST 2

DIRECTIONS: Each question or incomplete statement is followed by several suggested answers or completions. Select the one that BEST answers the question or completes the statement. *PRINT THE LETTER OF THE CORRECT ANSWER IN THE SPACE AT THE RIGHT.*

Questions 1-6.

DIRECTIONS: Questions 1 through 6, inclusive, should be answered ONLY according to the information given in the following passage.

There is no other service offered by a community in which there is such intimate contact with the individual citizen as in the refuse collection service. Because of this intimate contact, it is vitally important that each sanitation man in the service have the proper public relations attitude.

He should be imbued with a genuine desire to provide good service. This service should be impartial, performed in a neat and efficient manner, and the employee should be competent, willing, and efficient.

Every employee in the refuse collection service should be trained in contacting the public whether his job calls for contact in person, by telephone, or by letter. All requests for information and all complaints should be acknowledged promptly and courteously. If practicable, a personal contact should then be made. Later, if necessary, this should be followed up by a proper written reply. Decisions should be backed by the logic of operational problems rather than by flat recitals of codes, ordinances, or rules. But more important than the settling of complaints is the carrying out of the work in such a manner as to eliminate the causes of complaints in the beginning. The chief causes of complaints are the rough handling of containers, spillage of refuse, damage to lawns and shrubbery by collectors, and incomplete removal service. These complaints can be minimized by the training of personnel and by instilling in them a desire to do a good job. The training of drivers to operate their equipment properly is also important. The impression which city equipment makes on the citizen depends on its use as well as on its appearance. A reckless driver or an inconsiderate driver is not liked under any circumstance, but if he is driving a municipal vehicle, his offense is doubly magnified. A driver training program will pay dividends not only in improved public relations but in reduced costs.

1. According to the above passage, the MAIN reason why it is important for a sanitation man to have a good public relations attitude is that  1.____

    A. refuse collection affects the community's health
    B. his work will be improved
    C. he is in close touch with the private citizen
    D. he is offering an important community service

2. According to the above passage, after a complaint about the refuse collection service is acknowledged, it is desirable NEXT to  2.____

    A. make an investigation
    B. make a decision about the complaint

C.  interview the complainant in person
   D.  follow up with a letter

3. According to the above passage, if a sanitation man has to make a decision in answer to a complaint from a citizen, it would be BEST for him to explain to the complainant

   A.  why refuse collection operations make this decision necessary
   B.  the reason for the decision by referring to the appropriate rules
   C.  the local code which justifies the decision
   D.  how the cause of the complaint might have been eliminated in the Beginning

3.____

4. Based on the above passage, it is reasonable to assume that when a sanitation man is assigned to handle requests for information or complaints about the refuse collection service, he should

   A.  give first attention to complaints
   B.  give first attention to requests for information
   C.  handle both complaints and information requests quickly
   D.  handle first whatever he has the greatest number of

4.____

5. According to the above passage, the one of the following which does NOT seem to be a main source of complaints by the public about the refuse collection service is

   A.  some material put out for collection being left over
   B.  noise of collectors
   C.  dirtying of the collection area
   D.  damage to property

5.____

6. According to the above passage, the public's reaction to a poor driver is

   A.  the same no matter what vehicle he is driving
   B.  more severe if the vehicle involved is in poor condition
   C.  more severe if he turns out to be a municipal employee
   D.  more severe if he is operating city equipment

6.____

Questions 7-9.

DIRECTIONS:   Questions 7 through 9 should be answered ONLY on the basis of the following passage.

   A heavy snowfall may cause delays in the movement of trains and buses. People are often late for work when it snows. Both pedestrians and cars have accidents because of snow and ice. Pedestrians slip and fall. Cars skid and collide.

7. The above passage indicates that heavy snow

   A.  is a beautiful thing to see
   B.  may make the trains run late
   C.  gives temporary work to the unemployed
   D.  should be cleared from sidewalks within four hours

7.____

8. According to the above passage, snow and ice may cause cars to

   A.  slow down        B.  freeze        C.  stall        D.  skid

8.____

9. The above passage says that when it snows, 9.____

    A. children love to have snowball fights
    B. people are often late for work
    C. garbage collection is halted
    D. snow plows must be attached to garbage trucks

Questions 10-11.

DIRECTIONS: Questions 10 and 11 are to be answered ONLY on the basis of the following passage.

It would be unusual for a snowstorm to develop without warning. When a warning is received, sanitation men load the salt spreaders and attach plows to the trucks.

10. According to the passage, a snowstorm seldom develops 10.____

    A. without advance notice
    B. in the spring
    C. in the city
    D. without rain coming first

11. Once a snow warning is received, sanitation men prepare for the storm by 11.____

    A. removing plows from the trucks
    B. greasing and oiling the salt spreaders
    C. emptying the salt spreaders
    D. putting plows on the trucks

Questions 12-14.

DIRECTIONS: Questions 12 through 14 are to be answered ONLY on the basis of the following passage.

Helping to prevent accidents is the job of every worker. Foremen should be told about unsafe equipment right away. Workers should wear safe clothing. Knees should be bent when lifting, and help should be enlisted when picking up heavy objects.

12. The above passage says that helping to prevent accidents is the job of 12.____

    A. the foreman         B. the safety division
    C. management         D. every worker

13. Equipment that is not safe should be 13.____

    A. used with special care
    B. reported to the foreman right away
    C. marked with a red tag
    D. parked at the side of the road

14. When lifting very heavy objects, the worker should 14.____

    A. ask the foreman to see what is being done
    B. keep legs straight

C. always wear protective gloves
D. get help to assist him

Questions 15-17.

DIRECTIONS: Questions 15 through 17 are to be answered ONLY on the basis of the information in the following passage.

Sanitation men sometimes have to listen to complaints from the public. When an angry citizen complains, the supervisor should remember to stay calm. If possible, the complaint should be answered. If the supervisor cannot answer the complaint, the complainant should be referred to someone who can answer it.

15. Sanitation men who come into contact with the public sometimes have to 15._____

    A. sweep up trash
    B. shout at citizens
    C. listen to complaints
    D. help put out fires

16. If a citizen who is complaining to the worker is very angry, the worker should 16._____

    A. get angry
    B. stay calm
    C. ignore him
    D. none of the above

17. If the worker cannot answer the complaint, he should 17._____

    A. make up something that sounds logical
    B. ask a passer-by for the information
    C. tell the complainant who can give him the answer
    D. tell the complainant he does not know and walk away

Questions 18-19.

DIRECTIONS: Questions 18 and 19 are to be answered ONLY on the basis of the following passage.

The Department of Sanitation starts early in the month of May to prepare for snow expected during the following winter. It begins by fixing the snow removal equipment which was used during the winter. It is then usually kept busy with either snow removal or preparation for snow removal every month through the end of March.

18. According to the above passage, for how many months during the year is the Department of Sanitation busy with either snow removal or preparation for snow removal? 18._____

    A. 9   B. 10   C. 11   D. 12

19. According to the passage, in the month of May, the Department of Sanitation 19._____

    A. stores the snow removal equipment
    B. fixes the snow removal equipment
    C. equips the sanitation men
    D. collects the garbage piled up because of snow

Questions 20-22.

DIRECTIONS: Questions 20 through 22 are to be answered ONLY on the basis of the paragraph below.

In an open discussion designed to arrive at solutions to community problems, the person leading the discussion group should give the members a chance to make their suggestions before he makes his. He must not be afraid of silence. If he talks just to keep things going, he will find he can't stop, and good discussion will not develop. In other words, the more he talks, the more the group will depend on him. If he finds, however, that no one seems ready to begin the discussion, his best *opening* is to ask for definitions of terms which form the basis of the discussion. By pulling out as many definitions or interpretations as possible, he can get the group started *thinking out loud,* which is essential to good discussion.

20. According to the passage above, good group discussion is *most likely* to result if the person leading the discussion group

    A. keeps the discussion going by speaking whenever the group stops speaking
    B. encourages the group to depend on him by speaking more than any other group member
    C. makes his own suggestions before the group has a chance to make theirs
    D. encourages discussion by asking the group to interpret the terms to be discussed

21. According to the paragraph above, *thinking out loud* by the discussion group is

    A. *good* practice because *thinking out loud* is important to good discussion
    B. *poor* practice because group members should think out their ideas before discussing them
    C. *good* practice because it will encourage the person leading the discussion to speak more
    D. *poor* practice because it causes the group to fear silence during a Discussion

22. According to the paragraph above, the one of the following which is LEAST desirable at an open discussion is having

    A. silent periods during which none of the group members speaks
    B. differences of opinion among the group members concerning the definition of terms
    C. a discussion leader who uses *openings* to get the discussion started
    D. a discussion leader who provides all suggestions and definitions for the group

Questions 23-24.

DIRECTIONS: Questions 23 and 24 are to be answered ONLY on the basis of the paragraph below.

When a written report must be submitted by a foreman to his supervisor, the best rule is *the briefer the better.* Obviously, this can be carried to extremes since all necessary information must be included. However, the ability to write a satisfactory one-page report is an important communication skill. There are many types of reports a foreman must submit to his supervisor. One is the form report, which is printed and merely requires the foreman to fill in blanks. The greatest problem faced in completion of this report is accuracy and thoroughness. Another type of report is one that must be submitted regularly and systematically. This type of report is known as the periodic report.

23. According to the passage above, accuracy and thoroughness are the GREATEST problems in the completion of _____ reports.   23._____

    A. one-page    B. form    C. periodic    D. long

24. According to the passage above, a good written report from a foreman to his supervisor should GENERALLY be   24._____

    A. printed    B. periodic    C. brief    D. formal

Question 25.

DIRECTIONS: Question 25 is to be answered ONLY on the basis of the paragraph below.

Since metering reduces water waste considerably, daily operating costs are similarly reduced. Less water pumped means less expense for power to run pumps, less chemicals for treatment, less overall overhead and operating expense.

25. According to the above paragraph, the one of the following statements that is CORRECT is:   25._____

    A. Water is chemically treated in order to save power
    B. Water is chemically treated in order to save on overhead
    C. Metering of water means that more water must be pumped
    D. Metering of water results in less overall overhead and operating expenses

# KEY (CORRECT ANSWERS)

1. C          11. D
2. C          12. D
3. A          13. B
4. C          14. D
5. B          15. C

6. D          16. B
7. B          17. C
8. D          18. C
9. B          19. B
10. A         20. D

            21. A
            22. D
            23. B
            24. C
            25. D

# TEST 3

Questions 1-22.

DIRECTIONS: Each question consists of a statement. You are to indicate whether the statement is TRUE (T) or FALSE (F). *PRINT THE LETTER OF THE CORRECT ANSWER IN THE SPACE AT THE RIGHT.*

Questions 1-12.

DIRECTIONS: Questions 1 through 12 are to be answered ONLY on the basis of the information contained in the following paragraph.

### RESCUE BREATHING

Mouth-to-mouth, or rescue breathing, is the easiest, most efficient and quickest method of getting oxygen into a suffocating victim of drowning, heart attack, electrical shock, poisoning, or other cause of interruption of breathing. It is superior to other types of artificial respiration because the victim does not have to be moved, and the rescuer can continue for hours without exhaustion. No special equipment is needed.

Begin rescue breathing immediately. The victim's head should be lower than his body. Tilt his head back as far as possible so his jaw juts out. Keep the air passage to his lungs straight at all times. Open your mouth as wide as possible, and seal your lips over the adult victim's mouth or his nose and the child victim's mouth and nose. Blow in air until his chest rises. Remove your mouth and listen to him breathe out. Then blow again and fill his lungs.

For the first minute, blow thirty times into a child, then twenty times a minute. With an adult, blow twenty times for the first minute then ten to twelve times a minute. Do not stop breathing for the victim, however long it takes, until he begins breathing for himself — or is dead.

1. The fastest way to get oxygen into the lungs of a suffocating person is by mouth-to-mouth breathing.

2. The rescue breathing method of artificial respiration should be used only in cases of drowning.

3. Rescue breathing is not the only kind of artificial respiration.

4. The person who applies mouth-to-mouth breathing will not tire easily.

5. Special equipment used in rescue breathing should be kept handy at all times.

6. Rescue breathing should be commenced at the earliest possible moment.

7. The suffocating victim should be placed so that his body is not higher than his head.

8. In rescue breathing, the head of the victim should be bent forward so oxygen will be more easily forced into his lungs.

9. In mouth-to-mouth breathing, air may be blown into the victim's nose.

104

10. When rescue breathing is applied to children, air should be blown into the lungs thirty times during the first minute.

11. It is never necessary to continue rescue breathing for longer than about five minutes.

12. Mouth-to-mouth breathing is always successful in reviving the victim.

Questions 13-16.

DIRECTIONS: Questions 13 through 16 are to be answered ONLY on the basis of the information contained in the following paragraph.

Standardizing the size of a satisfactory refuse container may determine how often refuse is collected. A standard size is arrived at by considering the ease of handling the can and the average rate of accumulation of the refuse at the household. An excessive amount of refuse at the household should be avoided as it invariably leads to inferior sanitation practices.

13. The frequency of refuse collection may be influenced by the size of the refuse container.

14. Ease of handling a refuse can is a factor in arriving at a standard size for a refuse container.

15. The cause of poorer sanitation practices is invariably excessive piling up of refuse at the household.

16. Excessive production of refuse at the household should be prevented.

Questions 17-22.

DIRECTIONS: Questions 17 through 22 are to be answered ONLY on the basis of the information contained in the following paragraph.

It is possible for an inspection program of sanitation equipment to contribute toward the maximum utilization of equipment only if the inspections are properly scheduled, performed, and acted upon. This is so because the maximum utilization of equipment depends on a number of factors. A long life span for the equipment must be obtained by proper maintenance and repair. Organization and scheduling the manpower and equipment must be directed toward preventing the equipment from remaining unnecessarily idle. The maximum period of time for the use of any piece of motor equipment is that interval between the instant the equipment is received and the moment it becomes obsolete, the interval of availability. The purpose of an inspection program is to help expand the volume of work accomplished by equipment within the interval of availability, which in modern times is rapidly contracting.

17. If inspections of sanitation equipment are properly scheduled, performed, and acted upon, they insure maximum utilization of equipment.

18. To get a long life span for the equipment, proper maintenance and repair are necessary.

19. Maximum use of manpower is obtained when there is maximum use of equipment.

20. The longest period of time possible for the use of a piece of motor equipment is the time between the moment it becomes obsolete and the instant it is received.

21. The purpose of an equipment inspection program is to help increase the volume of work produced by the equipment from the time the equipment is received until the time it becomes obsolete.

22. In modern times, the maximum period of time for the use of any piece of motor equipment is rapidly shrinking.

Questions 23-25.

DIRECTIONS: Questions 23 through 25, inclusive, are to be answered in accordance with the following paragraph. Each question or statement is followed by several suggested answers or completions. Select the one that BEST answers the question or completes the statement. *PRINT THE LETTER OF THE CORRECT ANSWER IN THE SPACE AT THE RIGHT.*

You have been instructed to expedite the fabrication of three special sand spreader trucks using chassis that are available in the shop. All three trucks must be completed by November 1, 2007. Based on workload and available hours, the foreman of the body shop indicates that he could manufacture one complete sand spreader body per month, with one additional week required for mounting and securing each body to the available chassis. No work could begin on the body until the engines and hydraulic components, which would have to be purchased, were available for use. The Purchasing Department has promised the delivery of engines and hydraulic components three months after the order is placed. (Assume that all months have four weeks, and the same crew is doing the assembling and manufacturing.)

23. With reference to the above paragraph, the LATEST date that the engines and associated hydraulic components could be requisitioned in order to meet the specified deadline would be MOST NEARLY the end of the _____ week in _____ 2007.  23.____

   A. second; March  B. first; April
   C. first; May  D. first; June

24. With reference to the above paragraph, the date of completion of the first sand spreader truck, assuming that the Purchasing Department placed the order at the beginning of the second week in February 2007 and ultimate delivery of the engines and components was delayed by a month would be MOST NEARLY the end of the _____ week in _____ 2007.  24.____

   A. second; June  B. fourth; June
   C. second; July  D. fourth; July

25. With reference to the above paragraph, the date of completion of the last sand spreader truck, assuming that the Purchasing Department placed the order at the beginning of the second week in February 2007 and actual delivery of the engines and components was made two weeks early, would be MOST NEARLY the end of the _____ week in _____ 2007.  25.____

   A. second; August  B. first; September
   C. third; September  D. second; October

# KEY (CORRECT ANSWERS)

| | | | |
|---|---|---|---|
| 1. | T | 11. | F |
| 2. | F | 12. | F |
| 3. | T | 13. | T |
| 4. | T | 14. | T |
| 5. | F | 15. | F |
| 6. | T | 16. | F |
| 7. | F | 17. | F |
| 8. | F | 18. | T |
| 9. | T | 19. | F |
| 10. | T | 20. | T |

21. T
22. T
23. B
24. C
25. A

# REPORT WRITING

# EXAMINATION SECTION

# TEST 1

DIRECTIONS: Each question or incomplete statement is followed by several suggested answers or completions. Select the one that BEST answers the question or completes the statement. *PRINT THE LETTER OF THE CORRECT ANSWER IN THE SPACE AT THE RIGHT.*

1. Following are six steps that should be taken in the course of report preparation:
   I. Outlining the material for presentation in the report
   II. Analyzing and interpreting the facts
   III. Analyzing the problem
   IV. Reaching conclusions
   V. Writing, revising, and rewriting the final copy
   VI. Collecting data

   According to the principles of good report writing, the CORRECT order in which these steps should be taken is:
   A. VI, III, II, I, IV, V
   B. III, VI, II, IV, I, V
   C. III, VI, II, I, IV, V
   D. VI, II, III, IV, I, V

   1.____

2. Following are three statements concerning written reports:
   I. Clarity is generally more essential in oral reports than in written reports.
   II. Short sentences composed of simple words are generally preferred to complex sentences and difficult words.
   III. Abbreviations may be used whenever they are customary and will not distract the attention of the reader.

   Which of the following choices correctly classifies the above statements in to those which are valid and those which are not valid?
   A. I and II are valid, but III is not valid
   B. I is valid, but II and III are not valid.
   C. II and III are valid, but I is not valid.
   D. III is valid, but I and II are not valid.

   2.____

3. In order to produce a report written in a style that is both understandable and effective, an investigator should apply the principles of unit, coherence, and emphasis.
   The one of the following which is the BEST example of the principle of coherence is
   A. interlinking sentences so that thoughts flow smoothly
   B. having each sentence express a single idea to facilitate comprehension
   C. arranging important points in prominent positions so they are not overlooked
   D. developing the main idea fully to insure complete consideration

   3.____

109

4. Assume that a supervisor is preparing a report recommending that a standard work procedure be changed.
Of the following, the MOST important information that he should include in this report is
   A. a complete description of the present procedure
   B. the details and advantages of the recommended procedure
   C. the type and amount of retraining needed
   D. the percentage of men who favor the change

5. When you include in your report on an inspection some information which you have obtained from other individuals, it is MOST important that
   A. this information have no bearing on the work these other people are performing
   B. you do not report as fact the opinions of other individuals
   C. you keep the source of the information confidential
   D. you do not tell the other individuals that their statements will be included in your report

6. Before turning in a report of an investigator of an accident, you discover some additional information you did not know about when you wrote the report.
Whether or not you re-write your report to include this additional information should depend MAINLY on the
   A. source of this additional information
   B. established policy covering the subject matter of the report
   C. length of the report and the time it would take you to re-write it
   D. bearing this additional information will have on the conclusions in the report

7. The MOST desirable *first* step in the planning of a written report is to
   A. ascertain what necessary information is readily available in the files
   B. outline the methods you will employ to get the necessary information
   C. determine the objectives and uses of the report
   D. estimate the time and cost required to complete the report

8. In writing a report, the practice of taking up the least important points and the most important points last is a
   A. *good* technique since the final points made in a report will make the greatest impression on the reader
   B. *good* technique since the material is presented in a more logical manner and will lead directly to the conclusions
   C. *poor* technique since the reader's time is wasted by having to review irrelevant information before finishing the report
   D. *poor* technique since it may cause the reader to lose interest in the report and arrive at incorrect conclusions about the report

3 (#1)

9. Which one of the following serves as the BEST guideline for you to follow for effective written reports?
Keep sentences
   A. short and limit sentences to one thought
   B. short and use as many thoughts as possible
   C. long and limit sentences to one thought
   D. long and use as many thoughts as possible

9.____

10. One method by which a supervisor might prepare written reports to management is to begin with the conclusions, results, or summary, and to follow this with the supporting data.
The BEST reason why management may *prefer* this form of report is that
   A. management lacks the specific training to understand the data
   B. the data completely supports the conclusions
   C. time is saved by getting to the conclusions of the report first
   D. the data contains all the information that is required for making the conclusions

10.____

11. When making written reports, it is MOST important that they be
   A. well-worded            B. accurate as to the facts
   C. brief                  D. submitted immediately

11.____

12. Of the following, the MOST important reason for a supervisor to prepare good written reports is that
   A. a supervisor is rated on the quality of his reports
   B. decisions are often made on the basis of the reports
   C. such reports take less time for superiors to review
   D. such reports demonstrate efficiency of department operations

12.____

13. Of the following, the BEST test of a good report is whether it
   A. provides the information needed
   B. shows the good sense of the writer
   C. is prepared according to a proper format
   D. is grammatical and neat

13.____

14. When a supervisor writes a report, he can BEST show that he has a understanding of the subject of the report by
   A. including necessary facts and omitting nonessential details
   B. using statistical data
   C. giving his conclusions but not the data on which they are based
   D. using a technical vocabulary

14.____

15. Suppose you and another supervisor on the same level are assigned to work together on a report. You disagree strongly with one of the recommendations the other supervisor wants to include in the report but you cannot change his views.

15.____

111

Of the following, it would be BEST that
- A. you refuse to accept responsibility for the report
- B. you ask that someone else be assigned to this project to replace you
- C. each of you state his own ideas about this recommendation in the report
- D. you give in to the other supervisor's opinion for the sake of harmony

16. Standardized forms are often provided for submitting reports.
Of the following, the MOST important advantage of using standardized forms for reports is that
    - A. they take less time to prepare than individually written reports
    - B. the person making the report can omit information he considers unimportant
    - C. the responsibility for preparing these reports can be turned over to subordinates
    - D. necessary information is less likely to be omitted

16.____

17. A report which may BEST be classed as a *periodic* report is one which
    - A. requires the same type of information at regular intervals
    - B. contains detailed information which is to be retained in permanent records
    - C. is prepared whenever a special situation occurs
    - D. lists information in graphic form

17.____

18. In the writing of reports or letters, the ideas presented in a paragraph are usually of unequal importance and require varying degrees of emphasis.
All of the following are methods of placing extra stress on an idea EXCEPT
    - A. repeating it in a number of forms
    - B. placing it in the middle of the paragraph
    - C. placing it either at the beginning or at the end of a paragraph
    - D. underlining it

18.____

Questions 19-25.

DIRECTIONS: Questions 19 through 25 concern the subject of report writing and are based on the information and incidents described in the following paragraph. (In answering these questions, assume that the facts and incidents in the paragraph are true.)

On December 15, at 8 A.M., seven Laborers reported to Foreman Joseph Meehan in the Greenbranch Yard in Queens. Meehan instructed the men to load some 50-pound boxes of books on a truck for delivery to an agency building in Brooklyn. Meehan told the men that, because the boxes were rather heavy, two men should work together, helping each other lift and load each box. Since Michael Harper, one of the Laborers, was without a partner, Meehan helped him with the boxes for a while. When Meehan was called to the telephone in a nearby building, however, Harper decided to lift a box himself. He appeared able to lift the box, but, as he got the box halfway up, he cried out that he had a sharp pain in his back. Another Laborer, Jorge Ortiz, who was passing by, ran over to help Harper put the box down. Harper suddenly dropped the box, which fell on Ortiz' right foot. By this time, Meehan had come out of the building. He immediately helped get the box off Ortiz' foot and had both men lie down. Meehan covered the men with blankets and called an ambulance, which arrived a half hour later. At the hospital, the doctor said that the X-ray results showed that Ortiz' right foot was broken in three places.

19. What would be the BEST term to use in a report describing the injury of Jorge Ortiz?   19.____
    A. Strain    B. Fracture    C. Hernia    D. Hemorrhage

20. Which of the following would be the MOST accurate summary for the Foreman to put in his report of the incident?   20.____
    A. Ortiz attempted to help Harper carry a box which was too heavy for one person, but Harper dropped it before Ortiz got there.
    B. Ortiz tried to help Harper carry a box but Harper got a pain in his back and accidentally dropped the box on Ortiz' foot.
    C. Harper refused to follow Meehan's orders and lifted a box too heavy for him; he deliberately dropped it when Ortiz tried to help him carry it.
    D. Harper lifted a box and felt a pain in his back; Ortiz tried to help Harper put the box down but Harper accidentally dropped it on Ortiz' foot.

21. One of the Laborers at the scene of the accident was asked his version of the incident.   21.____
    Which information obtained from this witness would be LEAST important for including in the accident report?
    A. His opinion as to the cause of the accident
    B. How much of the accident he saw
    C. His personal opinion of the victims
    D. His name and address

22. What should be the MAIN objective of writing a report about the incident described in the above paragraph? To   22.____
    A. describe the important elements in the accident situation
    B. recommend that such Laborers as Ortiz be advised not to interfere in another's work unless given specific instructions
    C. analyze the problems occurring when there are not enough workers to perform a certain task
    D. illustrate the hazards involved in performing routine everyday tasks

23. Which of the following is information *missing* from the above passage but which *should* be included in a report of the incident? The   23.____
    A. name of the Laborer's immediate supervisor
    B. contents of the boxes
    C. time at which the accident occurred
    D. object or action that caused the injury to Ortiz' foot

24. According to the description of the incident, the accident occurred because   24.____
    A. Ortiz attempted to help Harper who resisted his help
    B. Harper failed to follow instructions given him by Meehan
    C. Meehan was not supervising his men as closely as he should have
    D. Harper was not strong enough to carry the box once he lifted it

25. Which of the following is MOST important for a foreman to avoid when writing up an official accident report?   25._____
    A. Using technical language to describe equipment involved in the accident
    B. Putting in details which might later be judged unnecessary
    C. Giving an opinion as to conditions that contributed to the accident
    D. Recommending discipline for employees who, in his opinion, caused the accident

---

## KEY (CORRECT ANSWERS)

| | | | |
|---|---|---|---|
| 1. | B | 11. | B |
| 2. | C | 12. | B |
| 3. | A | 13. | A |
| 4. | B | 14. | A |
| 5. | B | 15. | C |
| 6. | D | 16. | D |
| 7. | C | 17. | A |
| 8. | D | 18. | B |
| 9. | A | 19. | B |
| 10. | C | 20. | D |

| | |
|---|---|
| 21. | C |
| 22. | A |
| 23. | C |
| 24. | B |
| 25. | D |

# TEST 2

DIRECTIONS: Each question or incomplete statement is followed by several suggested answers or completions. Select the one that BEST answers the question or completes the statement. *PRINT THE LETTER OF THE CORRECT ANSWER IN THE SPACE AT THE RIGHT.*

1. Lieutenant X is preparing a report to submit to his commanding officer in order to get approval of a plan of operation he has developed.
   The report starts off with the statement of the problem and continues with the details of the problem. It contains factual information gathered with the help of field and operational personnel. It contains a final conclusion and recommendation for action. The recommendation is supplemented by comments from other precinct staff members on how the recommendations will affect their areas of responsibility. The report also includes directives and general orders ready for the commanding officer's signature. In addition, it has two statements of objections presented by two precinct staff members.
   Which one of the following, if any, is either an item that Lieutenant X should have included in his report and which is not mentioned above, or is an item which Lieutenant X improperly did include in his report?
   A. Considerations of alternative courses of action and their consequences should have been covered in the report.
   B. The additions containing undocumented objections to the recommended course of action should not have been included as part of the report.
   C. A statement on the qualifications of Lieutenant X, which would support his expertness in the field under consideration, should have been included in the report.
   D. The directives and general orders should not have been prepared and included in the report until the commanding officer had approved the recommendations.
   E. None of the above, since Lieutenant X's report was both proper and complete.

   1.____

2. During a visit to a section, the district supervisor criticizes the method being used by the assistant foreman to prepare a certain report and orders him to modify the method. This change ordered by the district supervisor is in direct conflict with the specific orders of the foreman.
   In this situation, it would be BEST for the assistant foreman to
   A. change the method and tell the foreman about the change at the first opportunity
   B. change the method and rely on the district supervisor to notify the foreman
   C. report the matter to the foreman and delay the preparation of the report
   D. ask the district supervisor to discuss the matter with the foreman but use the old method for the time being

   2.____

3. A department officer should realize that the MOST usual reason for writing a report is to
   A. give orders and follow up their execution
   B. establish a permanent record
   C. raise questions
   D. supply information

4. A very important report which is being prepared by a department officer will soon be due on the desk of the district supervisor. No typing help is available at this time for the officer.
   For the officer to write out this report in longhand in such a situation would be
   A. *bad*; such a report would not make the impression a typed report would
   B. *good*; it is important to get the report in on time
   C. *bad*; the district supervisor should not be required to read longhand reports
   D. *good*; it would call attention to the difficult conditions under which this section must work

5. In a well-written report, the length of each paragraph in the report should be
   A. varied according to the content
   B. not over 300 words
   C. pretty nearly the same
   D. gradually longer as the report is developed and written

6. A clerk in the headquarters office complains to you about the way in which you are filing out a certain report.
   It would be BEST for you to
   A. tell the clerk that you are following official procedures in filling out the report
   B. ask to be referred to the clerk's superior
   C. ask the clerk exactly what is wrong with the way in which you are filling out the report
   D. tell the clerk that you are following the directions of the district supervisor

7. The use of an outline to help in writing a report is
   A. *desirable*, in order to insure good organization and coverage
   B. *necessary*, so it can be used as an introduction to the report itself
   C. *undesirable*, since it acts as a straightjacket and may result in an unbalanced report
   D. *desirable*, if you know your immediate supervisor reads reports with extreme care and attention

8. It is advisable that a department officer do his paper work and report writing as soon as he has completed an inspection MAINLY because
   A. there are usually deadlines to be met
   B. it insures a steady work-flow
   C. he may not have time for this later
   D. the facts are then freshest in his mind

9. Before you turn in a report you have written of an investigation that you have made, you discover some additional information you didn't know about before. Whether or not you re-write the report to include this additional information should depend MAINLY on the
    A. amount of time remaining before the report is due
    B. established policy of the department covering the subject matter of the report
    C. bearing this information will have on the conclusions of the report
    D. number of people who will eventually review the report

9.____

10. When a supervisory officer submits a periodic report to the district supervisor, he should realize that the CHIEF importance of such a report is that it
    A. is the principal method of checking on the efficiency of the supervisor and his subordinates
    B. is something to which frequent reference will be made
    C. eliminates the need for any personal follow-up or inspection by higher echelons
    D. permits the district supervisor to exercise his functions of direction, supervision, and control better

10.____

11. Conclusions and recommendations are usually placed at the end rather than at the beginning of a report because
    A. the person preparing the report may decide to change some of the conclusions and recommendations before he reaches the end of the report
    B. they are the most important part of the report
    C. they can be judged better by the person to whom the report is sent after he reads the facts and investigators which come earlier in the report
    D. they can be referred to quickly when needed without reading the rest of the report

11.____

12. The use of the same method of record-keeping and reporting by all agency sections is
    A. *desirable*, MAINLY because it saves time in section operations
    B. *undesirable*, MAINLY because it kills the initiative of the individual section foreman
    C. *desirable*, MAINLY because it will be easier for the administrator to evaluate and compare section operations
    D. *undesirable*, MAINLY because operations vary from section to section and uniform record-keeping and reporting is not appropriate

12.____

13. The GREATEST benefit the section officer will have from keeping complete and accurate records and reports of section operations is that
    A. he will find it easier to run his section efficiently
    B. he will need less equipment
    C. he will need less manpower
    D. the section will run smoothly when he is out

13.____

14. You have prepared a report to your superior and are ready to send it forward. But on re-reading it, you think some parts are not clearly expressed and your superior ay have difficulty getting your point.
    Of the following, it would be BEST for you to
    A. give the report to one of your men to read, and if he has no trouble understanding it send it through
    B. forward the report and call your superior the next day to ask whether it was all right
    C. forward the report as is; higher echelons should be able to understand any report prepared by a section officer
    D. do the report over, re-writing the sections you are in doubt about

15. The BEST of the following statements concerning reports is that
    A. a carelessly written report may give the reader an impression of inaccuracy
    B. correct grammar and English are unimportant if the main facts are given
    C. every man should be required to submit a daily work report
    D. the longer and more wordy a report is, the better it will read

16. In writing a report, the question of whether or not to include certain material could be determined BEST by considering the
    A. amount of space the material will occupy in the report
    B. amount of time to be spent in gathering the material
    C. date of the material
    D. value of the material to the superior who will read the report

17. Suppose you are submitting a fairly long report to your superior.
    The one of the following sections that should come FIRST in this report is a
    A. description of how you gathered material
    B. discussion of possible objections to your recommendations
    C. plan of how your recommendations can be put into practice
    D. statement of the problem dealt with

Questions 18-20.

DIRECTIONS: A foreman is asked to write a report on the incident described in the following passage. Answer Questions 18 through 20 based on the following information.

On March 10, Henry Moore, a laborer, was in the process of transferring some equipment from the machine shop to the third floor. He was using a dolly to perform this task and, as he was wheeling the material through the machine shop, laborer Bob Greene called to him. As Henry turned to respond to Bob, he jammed the dolly into Larry Mantell's leg, knocking Larry down in the process and causing the heavy drill that Larry was holding to fall on Larry's foot. Larry started rubbing his foot and then, infuriated, jumped up and punched Henry in the jaw. The force of the blow drove Henry's head back against the wall. Henry did not fight back; he appeared to be dazed. An ambulance was called to take Henry to the hospital, and the ambulance attendant told the foreman that it appeared likely that Henry had suffered a concussion. Larry's injuries consisted of some bruises, but he refused medical attention.

18. An adequate report of the above incident should give as minimum information the names of the persons involved, the names of the witnesses, the date and the time that each event took place, and the
    A. names of the ambulance attendants
    B. names of all the employees working in the machine shop
    C. location where the accident occurred
    D. nature of the previous safety training each employee had been given

    18._____

19. The only one of the following which is NOT a fact is
    A. Bob called to Henry
    B. Larry suffered a concussion
    C. Larry rubbed his foot
    D. the incident took place in the machine shop

    19._____

20. Which of the following would be the MOST accurate summary of the incident for the foreman to put in his report of the accident?
    A. Larry Mantell punched Henry Moore because a drill fell on his foot and he was angry. Then Henry fell and suffered a concussion.
    B. Henry Moore accidentally jammed a dolly into Larry Mantell's foot, knocking Larry down. Larry punched Henry, pushing him into the wall and causing him to bang his head against the wall.
    C. Bob Greene called Henry Moore. A dolly than jammed into Larry Mantell and knocked him down. Larry punched Henry who tripped and suffered some bruises. An ambulance was called.
    D. A drill fell on Larry Mantell's foot. Larry jumped up suddenly and punched Henry Moore and pushed him into the wall. Henry may have suffered a concussion as a result of falling.

    20._____

Questions 21-25.

DIRECTIONS: Questions 21 through 25 are to be answered ONLY on the basis of the information provided in the following passage.

A written report is a communication of information from one person to another. It is an account of some matter especially investigated, however routine that matter may be. The ultimate basis of any good written report is facts, which become known through observation and verification. Good written reports may seem to be no more than general ideas and opinions. However, in such cases, the facts leading to these opinions were gathered, verified, and reported earlier, and the opinions are dependent upon these facts. Good style, proper form, and emphasis cannot make a good written report out of unreliable information and bad judgment; but, on the other hand, solid investigation and brilliant thinking are not likely to become very useful until they are effectively communicated to others. If a person's work calls for written reports, then his work is often no better than his written reports.

21. Based on the information in the above passage, it can be concluded that opinions expressed in a report should be
    A. based on facts which are gathered and reported
    B. emphasized repeatedly when they result from a special investigation
    C. kept to a minimum
    D. separated from the body of the report

    21._____

22. In the above passage, the one of the following which is mentioned as a way of establishing facts is
    A. authority
    B. communication
    C. reporting
    D. verification

    22._____

23. According to the above passage, the characteristic shared by ALL written reports is that they are
    A. accounts of routine matters
    B. transmissions of information
    C. reliable and logical
    D. written in proper form

    23._____

24. Which of the following conclusions can logically be drawn from the information given in the above passage?
    A. Brilliant thinking can make up for unreliable information in a report.
    B. One method of judging an individual's work is the quality of the written reports he is required to submit.
    C. Proper form and emphasis can make a good report out of unreliable information.
    D. Good written reports that seem to be no more than general ideas should be rewritten.

    24._____

25. Which of the following suggested titles would be MOST appropriate for this passage?
    A. Gathering and Organizing Facts
    B. Techniques of Observation
    C. Nature and Purpose of Reports
    D. Reports and Opinions: Differences and Similarities

    25._____

## KEY (CORRECT ANSWERS)

1. A
2. A
3. D
4. B
5. A

6. C
7. A
8. D
9. C
10. D

11. C
12. C
13. A
14. D
15. A

16. D
17. D
18. C
19. B
20. B

21. A
22. D
23. B
24. B
25. C

# TEST 3

DIRECTIONS: Each question or incomplete statement is followed by several suggested answers or completions. Select the one that BEST answers the question or completes the statement. *PRINT THE LETTER OF THE CORRECT ANSWER IN THE SPACE AT THE RIGHT.*

Questions 1-5.

DIRECTIONS: The following is an accident report similar to those used in departments for reporting accidents. Questions 1 through 5 are be answered using ONLY the information given in this report.

ACCIDENT REPORT

| **FROM:** John Doe | **DATE OF REPORT:** June 23 | |
|---|---|---|
| **TITLE:** Sanitation Worker | | |
| **DATE OF ACCIDENT:** June 22 time 3 AM PM | **CITY:** Metropolitan | |
| **PLACE:** 1489 Third Avenue | | |
| **VEHICLE NO. 1** | **VEHICLE NO. 2** | |
| **OPERATOR:** John Doe, Sanitation Worker Title | **OPERATOR:** Richard Roe | |
| **VEHICLE CODE NO:** 14-238 | **ADDRESS:** 498 High Street | |
| **LICENSE NO.:** 0123456 | **OWNER:** Henry Roe **ADDRESS:** 786 E.83 St. | **LIC. NO.:** 5N1492 |
| **DESCRIPTION OF ACCIDENT:** Light green Chevrolet sedan while trying to pass drove in to rear side of sanitation truck which had stopped to collect garbage. No one was injured but there was property damage. ||| 
| **NATURE OF DAMAGE TO PRIVATE VEHICLE:** Right front fender crushed, bumper bent |||
| **DAMAGE TO CITY VEHICLE:** Front of left rear fender pushed in. Paint scraped. |||
| **NAME OF WITNESS:** Frank Brown | **ADDRESS:** 48 Kingsway | |
| **SIGNATURE OF PERSON MAKING THIS REPORT** *John Doe* | **BADGE NO.:** 428 | |

1. Of the following, the one which has been omitted from this accident report is the
   A. location of the accident
   B. drivers of the vehicles involved
   C. traffic situation at the time of the accident
   D. owners of the vehicles involved

   1.____

2. The address of the driver of Vehicle No. 1 is not required because he
   A. is employed by the department    B. is not the owner of the vehicle
   C. reported the accident            D. was injured in the accident

   2.____

3. The report indicates that the driver of Vehicle No. 2 was PROBABLY
   A. passing on the wrong side of the truck
   B. not wearing his glasses
   C. not injured in the accident
   D  driving while intoxicated

   3.____

4. The number of people *specifically* referred to in this report is  4.____
   A. 3  B. 4  C. 5  D. 6

5. The license number of Vehicle No. 1 is  5.____
   A. 428  B. 5N1492  C. 14-238  D. 0123456

6. In a report of unlawful entry into department premises, it is LEAST important to include the  6.____
   A. estimated value of the property missing
   B. general description of the premises
   C. means used to get into the premises
   D. time and date of entry

7. In a report of an accident, it is LEAST important to include the  7.____
   A. name of the insurance company of the person injured in the accident
   B. probable cause of the accident
   C. time and place of the accident
   D. names and addresses of all witnesses of the accident

8. Of the following, the one which is NOT required in the preparation of a weekly functional expense report is the  8.____
   A. hourly distribution of the time by proper heading in accordance with the actual work performed
   B. signatures of officers not involved in the preparation of the report
   C. time records of the men who appear on the payroll of the respective locations
   D. time records of men working in other districts assigned to this location

## KEY (CORRECT ANSWERS)

| | | | |
|---|---|---|---|
| 1. | C | 5. | D |
| 2. | A | 6. | B |
| 3. | C | 7. | A |
| 4. | B | 8. | B |

# CLERICAL ABILITIES TEST

Clerical aptitude involves the ability to perceive pertinent detail in verbal or tabular material, to observe differences in copy, to proofread words and numbers, and to avoid perceptual errors in arithmetic computation.

NATURE OF THE TEST

Four types of clerical aptitude questions are presented in the Clerical Abilities Test. There are 120 questions with a short time limit. The test contains 30 questions on name and number checking, 30 on the arrangement of names in correct alphabetical order, 30 on simple arithmetic, and 30 on inspecting groups of letters and numbers. The questions have been arranged in groups or cycles of five questions of each type. The Clerical Abilities Test is primarily a test of speed in carrying out relatively simple clerical tasks. While accuracy on these tasks is important and will be taken into account in the scoring, experience has shown that many persons are so concerned about accuracy that they do the test more slowly than they should. Competitors should be cautioned that speed as well as accuracy is important to achieve a good score.

HOW THE TEST IS ADMINISTERED

Each competitor should be given a copy of the test booklet with sample questions on the cover page, an answer sheet, and a medium No. 2 pencil. Ten minutes are allowed to study the directions and sample questions and to answer the questions in the proper boxes on the two pages.
The separate answer sheet should be used for the test proper. Fifteen minutes are allowed for the test.

HOW THE TEST IS SCORED

The correct answers should be counted and recorded. The number of incorrect answers must also be counted because one-fourth of the number of incorrect answers is subtracted from the number of right answers. An omission is considered as neither a right nor a wrong answer. The score on this test is the number of right answers minus one-fourth of the number of wrong answers (fractions of one-half or less are dropped). For example, if an applicant had answered 89 questions correctly and 10 questions incorrectly, and had omitted 1 question, his score would be 87.

# EXAMINATION SECTION

DIRECTIONS: This test contains four kinds of questions. There are some of each kind on each page in the booklet. The time limit for the test will be announced by the examiner.
Use the special pencil furnished by the examiner in marking your answers on the separate answer sheet. For each question, there are five suggested answers. Decide which answer is correct, find the number of the question on the answer sheet, and make a solid black mark between the dotted lines just below the letter of your answer. If you wish to change your answer, erase the first mark completely, do not merely cross it out.

## SAMPLE QUESTIONS

In each line across the page there are three names or numbers that are much alike. Compare the three names or numbers and decide which ones are exactly alike. On the Sample Answer Sheet at the right, mark the answer
- A. if ALL THREE names or numbers are exactly ALIKE
- B. if only the FIRST and SECOND names or numbers are exactly ALIKE
- C. if only the FIRST and THIRD names or numbers are exactly ALIKE
- D. if only the SECOND and THIRD names or numbers are exactly ALIKE
- E. if ALL THREE names or numbers are DIFFERENT

| | | | |
|---|---|---|---|
| I. | Davis Hazen | David Hozen | David Hazen |
| II. | Lois Appel | Lois Appel | Lois Apfel |
| III. | June Allan | Jane Allan | Jane Allan |
| IV. | 10235 | 10235 | 10235 |
| V. | 32614 | 32164 | 32614 |

It will be to your advantage to learn what A, B, C, D, and E stand for. If you finish the sample questions before you are told to turn to the test, study them.

In the next group of sample questions, there is a name in a box at the left, and four other names in alphabetical order at the right. Find the correct space for the boxed name so that it will be in alphabetical order with the others, and mark the letter of that space as your answer.

VI. Jones, Jane

A. →
Goodyear, G.L.
B. →
Haddon, Harry
C. →
Jackson, Mary
D. →
Jenkins, William
E. →

VII. Kessler, Neilson

A. →
Kessel, Carl
B. →
Kessinger, D.J.
C. →
Kessler, Karl
D. →
Kessner, Lewis
E. →

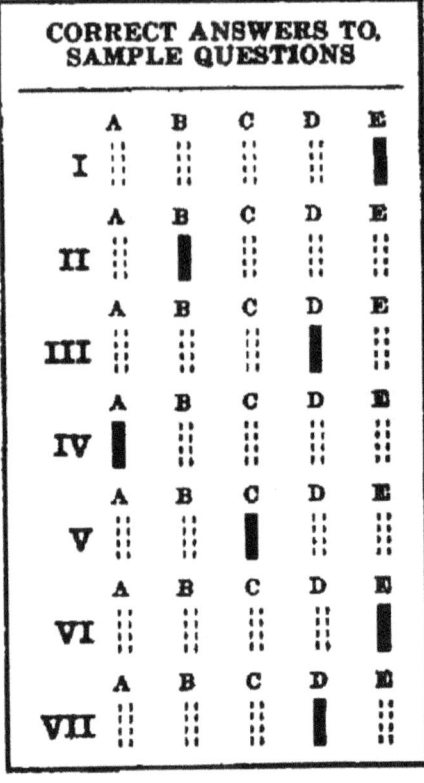

DIRECTIONS: In the following questions, complete the equation and find your answer among the list of suggested answers. Mark the Sample Answer Sheet A, B, C, or D for the answer you obtained; or if your answer is not among these, mark E for that question.

VIII. Add:  22
           +33

A. 44   B. 45   C. 54   D. 55   E. None of these

IX. Subtract:  24
              - 3

A. 20   B. 21   C. 27   D. 29   E. None of these

X. Multiply:  25
             x 5

A. 100   B. 115   C. 125   D. 135   E. None of these

XI. Divide: 6/̄1̄2̄6̄

    A. 20      B. 22      C. 24      D. 26      E. None of these

DIRECTIONS: There is one set of suggested answers for the next group of sample questions. Do not try to memorize these answers, because there will be a different set on each age in the test.

To find the answer to a question, find which suggested answer contains numbers and letters, all of which appear in the question. If no suggested answer fits, mark E for that question.

XII.   8 N K 9 G T 4 6

XIII.  T 9 7 Z 6 L 3 K

XIV.  Z 7 G K 3 9 8 N

XV.   3 K 9 4 6 G Z L

XVI.  Z N 7 3 8 K T 9

Suggested Answers
A = 7, 9, G, K
B = 8, 9, T, Z
C = 6, 7, K, Z
D = 6, 8, G, T
E = None of the above

After you have marked your answers to all the questions on the Sample Answer Sheets on this page and on the front page of the booklet, check them with the answers in the boxes marked Correct Answers To Sample Questions.

Questions 1-5.

In Questions 1 through 5, compare the three names or numbers, and mark
    A. if ALL THREE names or numbers are exactly ALIKE
    B. if only the FIRST and SECOND names or numbers are exactly ALIKE
    C. if only the FIRST and THIRD names or numbers are exactly ALIKE
    D. if only the SECOND and THIRD names or numbers are exactly ALIKE
    E. if ALL THREE names or numbers are DIFFERENT

| | | | |
|---|---|---|---|
| 1. | 5261383 | 5261383 | 5261338 |
| 2. | 8125690 | 8126690 | 8125609 |
| 3. | W.E. Johnston | W.E. Johnson | W.E. Johnson |
| 4. | Vergil L. Muller | Vergil L. Muller | Vergil L. Muller |

5.   Atherton R. Warde     Asheton R. Warde     Atherton P. Warde

Questions 6-10.

In Questions 6 through 10, find the correct place for the name in the box

6. | Hackett, Gerald |

A. →
  Habert, James
B. →
  Hachett, J.J.
C. →
  Hachetts, K. Larson
D. →
  Hachettson, Leroy
E. →

7. | Margenroth, Alvin |

A. →
  Margeroth, Albert
B. →
  Margestein, Dan
C. →
  Margestein, David
D. →
  Margue, Edgar
E. →

8. | Bobbitt, Olivier E. |

A. →
  Bobbitt, D. Olivier
B. →
  Bobbitt, Olivia B
C. →
  Bobbitt, Olivia H.
D. →
  Bobbitt, R. Olivia
E. →

9. | Mosley, Werner |

A. →
  Mosely, Albert J.
B. →
  Mosley, Alvin
C. →
  Mosley, S.M.
D. →
  Mozley, Vinson N.
E. →

10. Youmuns, Frank L.

A. → Youmons, Frank G.
B. → Youmons, Frank H.
C. → Youmons, Frank K.
D. → Youmons, Frank M.
E. →

Questions 11-15.

11. Add: 43
    +32

    A. 55   B. 65   C. 66   D. 75   E. None of these

12. Subtract: 83
    - 4

    A. 73   B. 79   C. 80   D. 89   E. None of these

13. Multiply: 41
    x 7

    A. 281   B. 287   C. 291   D. 297   E. None of these

14. Divide: 6/306

    A. 44   B. 51   C. 52   D. 60   E. None of these

15. Add: 37
    +15

    A. 42   B. 52   C. 53   D. 62   E. None of these

Questions 16-20.

In Questions 16 through 20, find which one of the suggested answers appears in that question.

16. 6 2 5 K 4 P T G

17. L 4 7 2 T 6 V K

18. 3 5 4 L 9 V T G

19. G 4 K 7 L 3 5 Z

SUGGESTED ANSWERS
A = 4, 5, K, T
B = 4, 7, G, K
C = 2, 5, G, L
D = 2, 7, L, T
E = None of the above

20. 4 K 2 9 N 5 T G

Questions 21-25.

In Questions 21 through 25, compare the three names or numbers, and mark
    A. if ALL THREE names or numbers are exactly ALIKE
    B. if only the FIRST and SECOND names or numbers are exactly ALIKE
    C. if only the FIRST and THIRD names or numbers are exactly ALIKE
    D. if only the SECOND and THIRD names or numbers are exactly ALIKE
    E. if ALL THREE names or numbers are DIFFERENT

| | | | |
|---|---|---|---|
| 21. | 2395890 | 2395890 | 2395890 |
| 22. | 1926341 | 1926347 | 1926314 |
| 23. | E. Owens McVey | E. Owen McVey | E. Owen McVay |
| 24. | Emily Neal Rouse | Emily Neal Rowse | Emily Neal Rowse |
| 25. | H. Merritt Audubon | H. Merriott Audubon | H. Merritt Audubon |

Questions 26-30.

In Questions 26 through 30, find the correct place for the name in the box.

26. Watters, N.O.

    A. →
        Waters, Charles L.
    B. →
        Waterson, Nina P.
    C. →
        Watson, Nora J.
    D. →
        Wattwood, Paul A.
    E. →

27. Johnston, Edward

    A. →
        Johnston, Edgar R.
    B. →
        Johnston, Edmond
    C. →
        Johnston, Edmund
    D. →
        Johnstone, Edmund A.
    E. →

28. | Rensch, Adeline |  A. →
    Ramsay, Amos
    B. →
    Remschel, Augusta
    C. →
    Renshaw, Austin
    D. →
    Rentzel, Becky
    E. →

29. | Schnyder, Maurice |  A. →
    Schneider, Martin
    B. →
    Schneider, Mertens
    C. →
    Schnyder, Newman
    D. →
    Schreibner, Norman
    E. →

30. | Freedenburg, C. Erma |  A. →
    Freedenberg, Emerson
    B. →
    Freedenberg, Erma
    C. →
    Freedenberg, Erma E.
    D. →
    Freedinberg, Erma F.
    E. →

Questions 31-35.

31. Subtract: 68
    − 47

    A. 10    B. 11    C. 20    D. 22    E. None of these

32. Multiply: 50
    × 8

    A. 400   B. 408   C. 450   D. 458   E. None of these

33. Divide: 9/180

    A. 20    B. 29    C. 30    D. 39    E. None of these

34. Add: 78
    + 63

    A. 131   B. 140   C. 141   D. 151   E. None of these

35. Add: 89
      -70

    A. 9        B. 18        C. 19        D. 29        E. None of these

Questions 36-40.

In Questions 36 through 40, find which one of the suggested answers appears in that question.

36.  9 G Z 3 L 4 6 N

37.  L 5 N K 4 3 9 V

38.  8 2 V P 9 L Z 5

39.  V P 9 Z 5 L 8 7

40.  5 T 8 N 2 9 V L

SUGGESTED ANSWERS
A = 4, 9, L, V
B = 4, 5, N, Z
C = 5, 8, L, Z
D = 8, 9, N, V
E = None of the above

Questions 41-45.

In Questions 41 through 45, compare the three names or numbers, and mark
    A. if ALL THREE names or numbers are exactly ALIKE
    B. if only the FIRST and SECOND names or numbers are exactly ALIKE
    C. if only the FIRST and THIRD names or numbers are exactly ALIKE
    D. if only the SECOND and THIRD names or numbers are exactly ALIKE
    E. if ALL THREE names or numbers are DIFFERENT

41.  6219354              621354              6219354

42.  2312793              2312793             2312793

43.  1065407              1065407             1065047

44.  Francis Ransdell     Frances Ramsdell    Francis Ramsdell

45.  Cornelius Detwiler   Cornelius Detwiler  Cornelius Detwiler

Questions 46-50.

In Questions 46 through 50, find the correct place for the name in the box.

46. | DeMattia, Jessica |

 A. →
 DeLong, Jesse
 B. →
 DeMatteo, Jessie
 C. →
 Derby, Jessie S.
 D. →
 DeShazo, L.M.
 E. →

47. | Theriault, Louis |

 A. →
 Therien, Annette
 B. →
 Therien, Elaine
 C. →
 Thibeault, Gerald
 D. →
 Thiebeault, Pierre
 E. →

48. | Gaston, M. Hubert |

 A. →
 Gaston, Dorothy M.
 B. →
 Gaston, Henry N.
 C. →
 Gaston, Isabel
 D. →
 Gaston, M. Melvin
 E. →

49. | SanMiguel, Carlos |

 A. →
 SanLuis, Juana
 B. →
 Santilli, Laura
 C. →
 Stinnett, Nellie
 D. →
 Stoddard, Victor
 E. →

50. | DeLaTour, Hall F. |

A. →
   DeLargy, Harold
B. →
   DeLathouder, Hilda
C. →
   Lathrop, Hillary
D. →
   LaTour, Hulbert E.
E. →

Questions 51-55.

51. Multiply: 62
              x 5

   A. 300    B. 310    C. 315    D. 360    E. None of these

52. Divide: 3/153

   A. 41     B. 43     C. 51     D. 53     E. None of these

53. Add: 47
        +21

   A. 58     B. 59     C. 67     D. 68     E. None of these

54. Subtract: 87
              - 42

   A. 34     B. 35     C. 44     D. 45     E. None of these

55. Multiply: 37
              x 3

   A. 91     B. 101    C. 104    D. 114    E. None of these

Questions 56-60.

For Questions 56 through 60, find which one of the suggested answers appears in that question.

56. N 5 4 7 T K 3 Z

57. 8 5 3 V L 2 Z N

58. 7 2 5 N 9 K L V

59. 9 8 L 2 5 Z K V

60. Z 6 5 V 9 3 P N

SUGGESTED ANSWERS
A = 3, 8, K, N
B = 5, 8, N, V
C = 3, 9, V, Z
D = 5, 9, K, Z
E = None of the above

Questions 61-65.

In Questions 61 through 65, compare the three names or numbers, and mark
    A.  if ALL THREE names or numbers are exactly ALIKE
    B.  if only the FIRST and SECOND names or numbers are exactly ALIKE
    C.  if only the FIRST and THIRD names or numbers are exactly ALIKE
    D.  if only the SECOND and THIRD names or numbers are exactly ALIKE
    E.  if ALL THREE names or numbers are DIFFERENT

61.  6452054                 6452654                6452054

62.  8501268                 8501268                8501286

63.  Ella Burk Newham     Ella Burk Newnham    Elena Burk Newnham

64.  Jno. K. Ravencroft      Jno. H. Ravencroft     Jno. H. Ravencoft

65.  Martin Wills Pullen    Martin Wills Pulen     Martin Wills Pullen

Questions 66-70.

In Questions 66 through 70, find the correct place for the name in the box.

66. | O'Bannon, M.J. |

    A. →
        O'Beirne, B.B.
    B. →
        Oberlin, E.L.
    C. →
        Oberneir, L.P.
    D. →
        O'Brian, S.F.
    E. →

67. | Entsminger, Jacob |

    A. →
        Ensminger, J.
    B. →
        Entsminger, J.A.
    C. →
        Entsminger, Jack
    D. →
        Entsminger, James
    E. →

68. | Iacone, Pete R. |
   A. →
      Iacone, Pedro
   B. →
      Iacone, Pedro M.
   C. →
      Iacone, Peter F.
   D. →
      Iascone, Peter W.
   E. →

69. | Sheppard, Gladys |
   A. →
      Shepard, Dwight
   B. →
      Shepard, F.H.
   C. →
      Shephard, Louise
   D. →
      Shepperd, Stella
   E. →

70. | Thackton, Melvin T. |
   A. →
      Thackston, Milton G.
   B. →
      Thackston, Milton W.
   C. →
      Thackston, Theodore
   D. →
      Thackston, Thomas G.
   E. →

Questions 71-75.

71. Divide: 7/357

   A. 51   B. 52   C. 53   D. 54   E. None of these

72. Add: 58
        +27

   A. 75   B. 84   C. 85   D. 95   E. None of these

73. Subtract: 86
            - 57

   A. 18   B. 29   C. 38   D. 39   E. None of these

74. Multiply: 68
    x 4

    A. 242      B. 264      C. 272      D. 274      E. None of these

75. Divide: 9/639

    A. 71       B. 73       C. 81       D. 83       E. None of these

Questions 76-80.

For Questions 76 through 80, find which one of the suggested answers appears in that question.

76.  6 Z T N 8 7 4 V

77.  V 7 8 6 N 5 P L

78.  N 7 P V 8 4 2 L

79.  7 8 G 4 3 V L T

80.  4 8 G 2 T N 6 L

SUGGESTED ANSWERS
A = 2, 7, L, N
B = 2, 8, T, V
C = 6, 8, L, T
D = 6, 7, N, V
E = None of the above

Questions 81-85.

In Questions 81 through 85, compare the three names or numbers, and mark
  A. if ALL THREE names or numbers are exactly ALIKE
  B. if only the FIRST and SECOND names or numbers are exactly ALIKE
  C. if only the FIRST and THIRD names or numbers are exactly ALIKE
  D. if only the SECOND and THIRD names or numbers are exactly ALIKE
  E. if ALL THREE names or numbers are DIFFERENT

| 81. | 3457988 | 3457986 | 3457986 |
| 82. | 4695682 | 4695862 | 4695682 |
| 83. | Stricklund Kanedy | Stricklund Kanedy | Stricklund Kanedy |
| 84. | Joy Harbor Witner | Joy Harloe Witner | Joy Harloe Witner |
| 85. | R.M.O. Uberroth | R.M.O. Uberroth | R.N.O. Uberroth |

Questions 86-90.

In Questions 86 through 90, find the correct place for the name in the box.

86. Dunlavey, M. Hilary

A. →
Dunleavy, Hilary G.
B. →
Dunleavy, Hilary K.
C. →
Dunleavy, Hilary S.
D. →
Dunleavy, Hilery W.
E. →

87. Yarbrough, Maria

A. →
Yabroudy, Margy
B. →
Yarboro, Marie
C. →
Yarborough, Marina
D. →
Yarborough, Mary
E. →

88. Prouty, Martha

A. →
Proutey, Margaret
B. →
Proutey, Maude
C. →
Prouty, Myra
D. →
Prouty, Naomi
E. →

89. Pawlowicz, Ruth M.

A. →
Pawalek, Edward
B. →
Pawelek, Flora G.
C. →
Pawlowski, Joan M.
D. →
Pawtowski, Wanda
E. →

90. | Vanstory, George |

A. →
   Vanover, Eva
B. →
   VanSwinderen, Floyd
C. →
   VanSyckle, Harry
D. →
   Vanture, Laurence
E. →

Questions 91-95

91. Add:  28
         +35

    A. 53    B. 62    C. 64    D. 73    E. None of these

92. Subtract:  78
              -69

    A. 7    B. 8    C. 18    D. 19    E. None of these

93. Multiply:  86
              x 6

    A. 492    B. 506    C. 516    D. 526    E. None of these

94. Divide:  8/648

    A. 71    B. 76    C. 81    D. 89    E. None of these

95. Add:  97
         +34

    A. 131    B. 132    C. 140    D. 141    E. None of these

Questions 96-100.

For Questions 96 through 100, find which one of the suggested answers appears in that question.

96. V 5 7 Z N 9 4 T

97. 4 6 P T 2 N K 9

98. 6 4 N 2 P 8 Z K

99. 7 P 5 2 4 N K T

100. K T 8 5 4 N 2 P

SUGGESTED ANSWERS
A = 2, 5, N, Z
B = 4, 5, N, P
C = 2, 9, P, T
D = 4, 9, T, Z
E = None of the above

Questions 101-105.

In Questions 101 through 105, compare the three names or numbers, and mark
   A. if ALL THREE names or numbers are exactly ALIKE
   B. if only the FIRST and SECOND names or numbers are exactly ALIKE
   C. if only the FIRST and THIRD names or numbers are exactly ALIKE
   D. if only the SECOND and THIRD names or numbers are exactly ALIKE
   E. if ALL THREE names or numbers are DIFFERENT

101. 1592514              1592574              1592574

102. 2010202              2010202              2010220

103. 6177396              6177936              6177396

104. Drusilla S. Ridgeley    Drusilla S. Ridgeley    Drusilla S. Ridgeley

105. Andrei I. Toumantzev    Andrei I. Tourmantzev   Andrei I. Toumantzov

Questions 106-110.

In Questions 106 through 110, find the correct place for the name in the box.

106. | Fitzsimmons, Hugh |

A. →
   Fitts, Harold
B. →
   Fitzgerald, June
C. →
   FitzGibbon, Junius
D. →
   FitzSimons, Martin
E. →

107. | D'Amato, Vincent |

A. →
   Daly, Steven
B. →
   D'Amboise, S. Vincent
C. →
   Daniel, Vail
D. →
   DeAlba, Valentina
E. →

108. | Schaeffer, Roger D. |

    A. →
       Schaffert, Evelyn M.
    B. →
       Schaffner, Margaret M.
    C. →
       Schafhirt, Milton G.
    D. →
       Shafer, Richard E.
    E. →

109. | White-Lewis, Cecil |

    A. →
       Whitelaw, Cordelia
    B. →
       White-Leigh, Nancy
    C. →
       Whitely, Rodney
    D. →
       Whitlock, Warren
    E. →

110. | VanDerHeggen, Don |

    A. →
       VanDemark, Doris
    B. →
       Vandenberg, H.E.
    C. →
       VanDercook, Marie
    D. →
       vanderLinden, Robert
    E. →

Questions 111-115.

111. Add:   75
         +49

    A. 124    B. 125    C. 134    D. 225    E. None of these

112. Subtract:   69
             - 45

    A. 14    B. 23    C. 24    D. 26    E. None of these

113. Multiply:   36
            x 8

    A. 246    B. 262    C. 288    D. 368    E. None of these

114. Divide: 8/328̄

    A. 31      B. 41      C. 42      D. 48      E. None of these

115. Multiply: 58
              x 9

    A. 472     B. 513     C. 521     D. 522     E. None of these

Questions 116-120.

For Questions 116 through 120, find which one of the suggested answers appears in that question.

116. Z 3 N P G 5 4 2

117. 6 N 2 8 G 4 P T

118. 6 N 4 T V G 8 2

119. T 3 P 4 N 8 G 2

120. 6 7 K G N 2 L 5

SUGGESTED ANSWERS:
A = 2, 3, G, N
B = 2, 6, N, T
C = 3, 4, G, K
D = 4, 6, K, T
E = None of the above

# KEY (CORRECT ANSWERS)

| | | | | | |
|---|---|---|---|---|---|
| 1. B | 21. A | 41. A | 61. C | 81. D | 101. D |
| 2. E | 22. E | 42. A | 62. B | 82. C | 102. B |
| 3. D | 23. E | 43. B | 63. E | 83. A | 103. C |
| 4. A | 24. D | 44. E | 64. E | 84. D | 104. A |
| 5. E | 25. C | 45. A | 65. C | 85. B | 105. E |
| 6. E | 26. D | 46. C | 66. A | 86. A | 106. D |
| 7. A | 27. D | 47. A | 667. D | 87. E | 107. B |
| 8. D | 28. C | 48. D | 68. C | 88. C | 108. A |
| 9. B | 29. C | 49. B | 69. D | 89. C | 109. C |
| 10. E | 30. D | 50. C | 70. E | 90. B | 110. D |
| 11. D | 31. E | 51. B | 71. A | 91. E | 111. A |
| 12. B | 32. A | 52. C | 72. C | 92. E | 112. C |
| 13. B | 33. A | 53. D | 73. B | 93. C | 113. C |
| 14. B | 34. C | 54. D | 74. C | 94. C | 114. B |
| 15. B | 35. C | 55. E | 75. A | 95. A | 115. D |
| 16. A | 36. E | 56. E | 76. D | 96. D | 116. A |
| 17. D | 37. A | 57. B | 77. D | 97. C | 117. B |
| 18. E | 38. C | 58. E | 78. A | 98. E | 118. B |
| 19. B | 39. C | 59. D | 79. E | 99. B | 119. A |
| 20. A | 40. D | 60. C | 80. C | 100. B | 120. E |

# NAME AND NUMBER COMPARISONS

## COMMENTARY

This test seeks to measure your ability and disposition to do a job carefully and accurately, your attention to exactness and preciseness of detail, your alertness and versatility in discerning similarities and differences between things, and your power in systematically handling written language symbols.

It is actually a test of your ability to do academic and/or clerical work, using the basic elements of verbal (qualitative) and mathematical (quantitative) learning—words and numbers.

## EXAMINATION SECTION

### TEST 1

DIRECTIONS: In each line across the page there are three names or numbers that are much alike. Compare the three names or numbers and decide which ones are exactly alike. *PRINT IN THE SPACE AT THE RIGHT THE LETTER:*
  A. if all THREE names or numbers are exactly alike
  B. if only the FIRST and SECOND names or numbers are ALIKE
  C. if only the FIRST and THIRD names or numbers are alike
  D. if only the SECOND or THIRD names or numbers are alike
  E. if ALL THREE names or numbers are DIFFERENT

| | | | | |
|---|---|---|---|---|
| 1. | Davis Hazen | David Hozen | David Hazen | 1.____ |
| 2. | Lois Appel | Lois Appel | Lois Apfel | 2.____ |
| 3. | June Allan | Jane Allan | Jane Allan | 3.____ |
| 4. | 10235 | 10235 | 10235 | 4.____ |
| 5. | 32614 | 32164 | 32614 | 5.____ |

### TEST 2

| | | | | |
|---|---|---|---|---|
| 1. | 2395890 | 2395890 | 2395890 | 1.____ |
| 2. | 1926341 | 1926347 | 1926314 | 2.____ |
| 3. | E. Owens McVey | E. Owen McVey | E. Owen McVay | 3.____ |
| 4. | Emily Neal Rouse | Emily Neal Rowse | Emily Neal Rowse | 4.____ |
| 5. | H. Merritt Audubon | H. Merriott Audubon | H. Merritt Audubon | 5.____ |

2

## TEST 3

| | | | | |
|---|---|---|---|---|
| 1. | 6219354 | 6219354 | 6219354 | 1.____ |
| 2. | 231793 | 2312793 | 2312793 | 2.____ |
| 3. | 1065407 | 1065407 | 1065047 | 3.____ |
| 4. | Francis Ransdell | Frances Ramsdell | Francis Ramsdell | 4.____ |
| 5. | Cornelius Detwiler | Cornelius Detwiler | Cornelius Detwiler | 5.____ |

## TEST 4

| | | | | |
|---|---|---|---|---|
| 1. | 6452054 | 6452564 | 6542054 | 1.____ |
| 2. | 8501268 | 8501268 | 8501286 | 2.____ |
| 3. | Ella Burk Newham | Ella Burk Newnham | Elena Burk Newnham | 3.____ |
| 4. | Jno. K. Ravencroft | Jno. H. Ravencroft | Jno. H. Ravencoft | 4.____ |
| 5. | Martin Wills Pullen | Martin Wills Pulen | Martin Wills Pullen | 5.____ |

## TEST 5

| | | | | |
|---|---|---|---|---|
| 1. | 3457988 | 3457986 | 3457986 | 1.____ |
| 2. | 4695682 | 4695862 | 4695682 | 2.____ |
| 3. | Stricklund Kaneydy | Sticklund Kanedy | Stricklund Kanedy | 3.____ |
| 4. | Joy Harlor Witner | Joy Harloe Witner | Joy Harloe Witner | 4.____ |
| 5. | R.M.O. Uberroth | R.M.O. Uberroth | R.N.O. Uberroth | 5.____ |

## TEST 6

| | | | |
|---|---|---|---|
| 1. | 1592514 | 1592574 | 1592574 | 1.____ |
| 2. | 2010202 | 2010202 | 2010220 | 2.____ |
| 3. | 6177396 | 6177936 | 6177396 | 3.____ |
| 4. | Drusilla S. Ridgeley | Drusilla S. Ridgeley | Drusilla S. Ridgeley | 4.____ |
| 5. | Andrei I. Tooumantzev | Andrei I. Tourmantzev | Andrei I. Toumantzov | 5.____ |

## TEST 7

| | | | |
|---|---|---|---|
| 1. | 5261383 | 5261383 | 5261338 | 1.____ |
| 2. | 8125690 | 8126690 | 8125609 | 2.____ |
| 3. | W.E. Johnston | W.E. Johnson | W.E. Johnson | 3.____ |
| 4. | Vergil L. Muller | Vergil L. Muller | Vergil L. Muller | 4.____ |
| 5. | Atherton R. Warde | Asheton R. Warde | Atherton P. Warde | 5.____ |

## TEST 8

| | | | |
|---|---|---|---|
| 1. | 013469.5 | 023469.5 | 02346.95 | 1.____ |
| 2. | 33376 | 333766 | 333766 | 2.____ |
| 3. | Ling-Temco-Vought | Ling-Tenco-Vought | Ling-Temco Vought | 3.____ |
| 4. | Lorilard Corp. | Lorillard Corp. | Lorrilard Corp. | 4.____ |
| 5. | American Agronomics Corporation | American Agronomics Corporation | American Agronomic Corporation | 5.____ |

4

## TEST 9

| | | | | | |
|---|---|---|---|---|---|
| 1. | 436592864 | 436592864 | 436592864 | 1.____ |
| 2. | 197765123 | 197755123 | 197755123 | 2.____ |
| 3. | Dewaay Cortvriendt International S.A. | Deway Cortvriendt International S.A. | Deway Corturiendt International S.A. | 3.____ |
| 4. | Crédit Lyonnais | Crèdit Lyonnais | Crèdit Lyonais | 4.____ |
| 5. | Algemene Bank Nederland N.V. | Algamene Bank Nederland N.V. | Algemene Bank Naderland N.V. | 5.____ |

## TEST 10

| | | | | | |
|---|---|---|---|---|---|
| 1. | 00032572 | 0.0032572 | 00032522 | 1.____ |
| 2. | 399745 | 399745 | 398745 | 2.____ |
| 3. | Banca Privata Finanziaria S.p.A. | Banca Privata Finanzaria S.P.A. | Banca Privata Finanziaria S.P.A. | 3.____ |
| 4. | Eastman Dillon, Union Securities & Co. | Eastman Dillon, Union Securities Co. | Eastman Dillon, Union Securities & Co. | 4.____ |
| 5. | Arnhold and S. Bleichroeder, Inc. | Arnhold & S. Bleichroeder, Inc. | Arnold and S. Bleichroeder, Inc. | 5.____ |

# TEST 11

DIRECTIONS: Answer the questions below on the basis of the following instructions: For each such numbered set of names, addresses, and numbers listed in Columns I and II, select your answer from the following options:
- A. The names in Columns I and II are different
- B. The addresses in Columns I and II are different
- C. The numbers in Columns I and II are different
- D. The names, addresses and numbers are identical

1. Francis Jones　　　　　　　　　　　Francis Jones　　　　　　　　　　　1._____
   62 Stately Avenue　　　　　　　　　62 Stately Avenue
   96-12446　　　　　　　　　　　　　 96-21446

2. Julio Montez　　　　　　　　　　　 Julio Montez　　　　　　　　　　　 2._____
   19 Ponderosa Road　　　　　　　　　19 Ponderosa Road
   56-73161　　　　　　　　　　　　　 56-71361

3. Mary Mitchell　　　　　　　　　　　Mary Mitchell　　　　　　　　　　　3._____
   2314 Melbourne Drive　　　　　　　 2314 Melbourne Drive
   68-92172　　　　　　　　　　　　　 68-92172

4. Harry Patterson　　　　　　　　　　Harry Patterson　　　　　　　　　　4._____
   25 Dunne Street　　　　　　　　　　25 Dunne Street
   14-33430　　　　　　　　　　　　　 14-34330

5. Patrick Murphy　　　　　　　　　　 Patrick Murphy　　　　　　　　　　 5._____
   171 West Hosmer Street　　　　　　 171 West Hosmer Street
   93-81214　　　　　　　　　　　　　 93-18214

## TEST 12

1. August Schultz　　　　　August Schultz　　　　　1.____
   816 St. Clair Avenue　　　816 St. Claire Avenue
   53-40149　　　　　　　　53-40149

2. George Taft　　　　　　George Taft　　　　　　2.____
   72 Runnymede Street　　72 Runnymede Street
   47-04033　　　　　　　　47-04023

3. Angus Henderson　　　Angus Henderson　　　3.____
   1418 Madison Street　　1418 Madison Street
   81-76375　　　　　　　　81-76375

4. Carolyn Mazur　　　　　Carolyn Mazur　　　　　4.____
   12 Rivenlew Road　　　12 Rivervane Road
   38-99615　　　　　　　　38-99615

5. Adele Russell　　　　　Adela Russell　　　　　5.____
   1725 Lansing Lane　　　1725 Lansing Lane
   72-91962　　　　　　　　72-91962

# TEST 13

DIRECTIONS: The following questions are based on the instructions given below. In each of the following questions, the 3-line name and address in Column I is the master-list entry, and the 3-line entry in Column II is the information to be checked against the master list.
If there is one line that is NOT exactly alike, mark your answer A.
If there are two lines NOT exactly alike, mark your answer B.
If there are three lines NOT exactly alike, mark your answer C.
If the lines ALL are exactly alike, mark your answer D.

1. Jerome A. Jackson　　　　　　　Jerome A. Johnson　　　　　　1.____
   1243 14th Avenue　　　　　　　　1234 14th Avenue
   New York, N.Y. 10023　　　　　　New York, N.Y. 10023

2. Sophie Strachtheim　　　　　　　Sophie Strachtheim　　　　　　2.____
   33-28 Connecticut Ave.　　　　　33-28 Connecticut Ave.
   Far Rockaway, N.Y. 11697　　　　Far Rockaway, N.Y. 11697

3. Elisabeth NT. Gorrell　　　　　 Elizabeth NT. Correll　　　　　3.____
   256 Exchange St　　　　　　　　　256 Exchange St.
   New York, N.Y. 10013　　　　　　New York, N.Y. 10013

4. Maria J. Gonzalez　　　　　　　 Maria J. Gonzalez　　　　　　　4.____
   7516 E. Sheepshead Rd.　　　　　7516 N. Shepshead Rd.
   Brooklyn, N.Y. 11240　　　　　　Brooklyn, N.Y. 11240

5. Leslie B. Brautenweiler　　　　 Leslie B. Brautenwieler　　　　5.____
   21-57A Seller Terr.　　　　　　 21-75ASeiler Terr.
   Flushing, N.Y. 11367　　　　　　Flushing, N.J. 11367

## KEY (CORRECT ANSWERS)

| TEST 1 | TEST 2 | TEST 3 | TEST 4 | TEST 5 | TEST 6 | TEST 7 |
|--------|--------|--------|--------|--------|--------|--------|
| 1. E   | 1. A   | 1. A   | 1. E   | 1. D   | 1. D   | 1. B   |
| 2. B   | 2. E   | 2. A   | 2. B   | 2. C   | 2. B   | 2. E   |
| 3. D   | 3. E   | 3. B   | 3. E   | 3. E   | 3. C   | 3. D   |
| 4. A   | 4. D   | 4. E   | 4. E   | 4. D   | 4. A   | 4. A   |
| 5. C   | 5. C   | 5. A   | 5. C   | 5. B   | 5. E   | 5. E   |

| TEST 8 | TEST 9 | TEST 10 | TEST 11 | TEST 12 | TEST 13 |
|--------|--------|---------|---------|---------|---------|
| 1. E   | 1. A   | 1. E    | 1. C    | 1. B    | 1. B    |
| 2. D   | 2. D   | 2. B    | 2. C    | 2. C    | 2. D    |
| 3. E   | 3. E   | 3. E    | 3. D    | 3. D    | 3. A    |
| 4. E   | 4. E   | 4. C    | 4. C    | 4. B    | 4. A    |
| 5. B   | 5. E   | 5. E    | 5. C    | 5. A    | 5. C    |

# ARITHMETICAL REASONING

## EXAMINATION SECTION
### TEST 1

DIRECTIONS: Each question or incomplete statement is followed by several suggested answers or completions. Select the one that BEST answers the question or completes the statement. *PRINT THE LETTER OF THE CORRECT ANSWER IN THE SPACE AT THE RIGHT.*

Questions 1-4.

DIRECTIONS: Answer Questions 1 through 4 by performing the operation required (addition or subtraction).

1. Add: 10,487
   + 145

   A. 10,342  B. 10,622  C. 10,632  D. 10,652

2. Add: 26,836
   + 87

   A. 26,749  B. 26,923  C. 26,943  D. 26,973

3. Subtract: 83,204
   -83.075

   A. 109  B. 129  C. 139  D. 144

4. Subtract: 19,095
   -19,029

   A. 66  B. 74  C. 79  D. 86

5. If the mileage indicator on your truck reads 14,382 at the beginning of the day, and it reads 14,431 at the end of the day, the number of miles that the truck has been driven that day is

   A. 29  B. 34  C. 39  D. 49

6. On a certain day, your truck makes three trips to the dumping area and dumps 5.5 tons, 6.3 tons, and 4.8 tons of trash.
   The TOTAL number of tons of trash that the truck has dumped that day is

   A. 15.0  B. 15.6  C. 16.0  D. 16.6

7. During one winter, there were 29 snowfalls with a total snow accumulation for the season of 57.6 inches. The next winter, there were 15 snowfalls with a total snow accumulation for the season of 7.9 inches.
The average snow accumulation per snowfall for the two winters combined was MOST NEARLY _____ inch(es).

   A. 1.00   B. 1.25   C. 1.50   D. 1.75

8. In District A, 1/6 of the sanitation work force took all its vacation in June, 1/3 of the force took all its vacation in July, and 1/4 took all its vacation in August. What part of the total sanitation work force of the district does this represent?

   A. 3/4   B. 7/12   C. 2/5   D. 3/13

9. In a four-year period, the Department of Sanitation used 314,997 tons of salt for snow removal. The first year, 79,651 tons were used. The second year, the Department used 6,592 tons less than the first year. In the third year, 11,981 tons of salt more were used than were used in the second year.
The number of tons of salt used in the fourth year was MOST NEARLY

   A. 77,275   B. 77,250   C. 77,225   D. 77,200

10. Suppose that the number of occupancies that the Department of Sanitation collects from in 6 different sections of the city are, respectively, 1,837, 962, 12,105, 4,923, 26,702, and 3,819.
The total number of occupancies that the Department must collect from in these 6 sections is MOST NEARLY

    A. 50,355   B. 50,350   C. 50,345   D. 50,340

11. A rectangular box measures 6 feet by 2 1/2 feet.
If the box is 3 feet deep, the cubic volume of the box is MOST NEARLY _____ cubic inches.

    A. 78,000   B. 41,000   C. 4,500   D. 138

12. Following is a list of symbols and their meanings:
    DSL = average loads per hour received from Department of Sanitation
    DST = total tons per day received from Department of Sanitation
    OL  = total loads per day received from others
    OT  = average tons per hour received from others

    Based on the above, which one of the following formulas will give the average tons per load received at an incinerator plant?

    A. $\dfrac{(24 \times DSL + OL)}{(DST + 24 \times OT)}$
    B. $\dfrac{(DST + OT)}{(24 \times DSL + OL)}$
    C. $\dfrac{(DST + 24 \times OT)}{(24 \times DSL + OL)}$
    D. $\dfrac{DST + 24 \times OT}{24 \times DSL + 24 \times OL}$

13. Assume that you are required to assist in the evaluation of a new piece of sanitation equipment that is powered by a diesel engine. The following data are available to you: fuel consumption is 0.6 pounds of fuel per hour per horsepower, 40 horsepower is required to meet the load, the fuel weighs 7 pounds per gallon.
Assuming 6 hours of operation per day, the number of gallons of fuel required is MOST NEARLY _____ gallons per day.

    A. 13        B. 20        C. 46        D. 100

14. Assume you are determining, from a large scale map (1/2 inch = 1/4 mile), the number of curb miles per man day for a mechanical sweeper. As you measure map distance, your notes show 10 1/8 inches, 8 3/4 inches, and 7 1/2 inches for the entire route.
The total curb miles is MOST NEARLY

    A. 6.7       B. 13.2      C. 14.5      D. 18.1

15. The total area, in square feet, of the following rooms:

    | Room | Square Feet |
    |------|-------------|
    | 201  | 1,196       |
    | 202  | 1,196       |
    | 203  | 827         |
    | 204  | 827         |

    is MOST NEARLY

    A. 3,000     B. 4,000     C. 5,000     D. 6,000

16. The AVERAGE area of the rooms listed in the preceding question is _____ of the total.

    A. 1/4       B. 1/3       C. 1/2       D. 3/4

17. The Public Relations Office's budget was $10,000.00 in 2012. Their 2013 budget was 5% higher than that of 2012, and their 2014 budget was 10% higher than that of 2013. The Office's budget for 2014 is

    A. $10,550   B. $11,150   C. $11,550   D. $12,050

18. The city recently purchased three pieces of machinery for use at a sanitation garage. One machine cost $1,739.55, the second machine cost $6,284.00. The total cost for all three machines was $12,721.00.
How much did the third machine cost?

    A. $4,607.55  B. $4,697.45  C. $4,797.55  D. $4,798.45

9. An Emergency Sanitation Aide is paid at the rate of $7.20 per hour. He worked 45 hours in one week and was paid double time for 3 of the 45 hours worked during this week. What was his TOTAL gross earnings for the week?

    A. $336.90   B. $345.60   C. $378.90   D. $465.60

20. Assuming that it requires 6 man-days to replace a sidewalk 4 feet wide x 120 feet long, then a similar sidewalk 8 feet wide x 78 feet long would require MOST NEARLY _____ man-days.

    A. 6  B. 8  C. 10  D. 14

20._____

---

## KEY (CORRECT ANSWERS)

| | | | |
|---|---|---|---|
| 1. | C | 11. | A |
| 2. | B | 12. | C |
| 3. | B | 13. | B |
| 4. | A | 14. | B |
| 5. | D | 15. | B |
| 6. | D | 16. | A |
| 7. | C | 17. | C |
| 8. | A | 18. | B |
| 9. | B | 19. | B |
| 10. | B | 20. | B |

# SOLUTIONS TO PROBLEMS

1. 10,487 + 145 = 10,632

2. 26,836 + 87 = 26,923

3. 83,204 - 83,075 = 129

4. 19,095 - 19,029 = 66

5. 14,431 - 14,382 = 49 miles

6. 5.5 +6.3 +4.8 =16.6 tons of trash

7. (57.6+7.9) ÷ (29+15) ≈ 1.50 in. per snowfall

8. $\frac{1}{6}+\frac{1}{3}+\frac{1}{4}=\frac{9}{12}=\frac{3}{4}$

9. 4th year usage = 314,997 - (79,651+73,059+85,040) = 77,247, or about 77,250 tons of salt

10. 1837 + 962 + 12,105 + 4923 + 26,702 + 3819 = 50,348   50,350

11. (72")(30")(36n) = 77,760 cu.in. ≈ 78,000 cu.in.

12. Average tons/load = (DST+24.OT) (24.DSL+OL)
    Note:  24.DSL = total loads per day received by DST
           24.OT = total tons per day received by others

13. (.6)(40)(6) = 144. Then, 144  7 ≈ 20.57   20 gallons

14. $10\frac{1}{8}" + 8\frac{3}{4}" + 7\frac{1}{2}" = 26\frac{3}{8}"$.  Then, $26\frac{3}{8}" \div \frac{1}{2}" = 52.75$
    Finally, (52.75)(1/4 mi.) ≈ 13.2 miles

15. 1196 + 1196 + 827 + 827 = 4046 sq. ft.   4000 sq.ft.

16. 4046 ÷ 4 = 1011.5, and 1011.5 must be 1/4 of the total sq.ft.

17. For 2014, the budget was ($10,000)(1.05)(1.10) = $11,550

18. $12,721 - $1739.55 - $6284 = $4697.45

19. ($7.20X42) + ($14.40X3) = $345.60

20. (4')(120') = 480 sq.ft., (8')(78') = 624 sq.ft. Then, we have $(6)(\frac{624}{480}) = 7.8 \approx$ 8 man-days

# TEST 2

DIRECTIONS: Each question consists of a statement. You are to indicate whether the statement is TRUE (T) or FALSE (F). *PRINT THE LETTER OF THE CORRECT ANSWER IN THE SPACE AT THE RIGHT.*

1. If a section had 48 miles of street to plow after a snowstorm and 9 plows are used, each plow would cover an average of 4 miles.  1.____

2. If a crosswalk plow engine is run 5 minutes a day for ten days in a given month, it would run one hour in the course of this month.  2.____

3. If the department uses 1,500 men in manual street cleaning and half as many more to load and drive trucks, the total number used is 2,200 men.  3.____

4. If an inspector issued 186 summonses in the course of 7 hours, his hourly average was 25 summonses issued.  4.____

5. If an inspector issued 186 summonses, one hundred were issued to first offenders, then there were 86 summonses issued to other than first offenders.  5.____

6. If one length of hose is 50 feet, six lengths equal 250 feet.  6.____

7. If the Department has 2 officers to every 18 men, the ratio is 1 to 9.  7.____

8. A street measuring 200' by 36' from curb to curb has an area of 800 square yards.  8.____

9. A ton pick-up truck will hold at least 2,000 lbs.  9.____

10. An employee who works from 6 P.M. to 4 A.M. the following morning works a total of 8 hours.  10.____

11. A truck body measuring 5 1/2 feet by 1 1/2 feet by 8 feet has a capacity of 66 cubic feet.  11.____

12. A sanitation truck averaging 18 miles per hour travels approximately 6 miles in 20 minutes.  12.____

13. A sanitation man born July 20, 1988 was 21 years and 22 days old on August 11, 2009.  13.____

14. If 231 cubic inches equal one gallon, then a 2J gallon fire extinguisher measures about 577.5 cubic inches.  14.____

15. If a scraper costs $1.87, then 100 scrapers will cost $18.70.  15.____

16. A loaded truck weighs 5,400 pounds. If the truck weighs twice as much as the load, the load weighs 1,800 pounds.  16.____

17. If eight men are needed to sweep a particular area in 6 hours, it would only take six men to sweep this area in 8 hours.  17.____

18. If a collection truck travels a half mile in 10 minutes, its speed is 15 miles per hour.  18.____

19. If twelve cans of sweepings fill a truck which can hold 1 1/2 tons, three cans of sweepings will fill a truck holding 1/2 ton.  19.____

20. The capacity of the body of a hired truck which is six feet wide, ten feet long, and six feet high is the same as one which measures six feet by twelve feet by five feet.   20._____

21. The sum of 2,345 and 4,483 is 6,882.   21._____

22. One-fifth of 295 is 59.   22._____

23. The difference between 2,876 and 1,453 is 1,423.   23._____

24. If each of 5 sections has 15 solar cans, the total of all five sections is 75 cans.   24._____

25. If there are 245 sections in the city, the average number of sections for each of the 5 counties is 49 sections.   25._____

26. If three men working at the same rate of speed finish a job in 4 1/2 hours, then two of them could do the job in 6 3/4 hours.   26._____

27. If a typist shares four boxes of envelopes with four other typists, each will have one box of envelopes.   27._____

28. An article bought for $100 must be sold for $125 in order to make a profit of 20% of the selling price.   28._____

29. 1/2 of 1/8 is 1/4.   29._____

30. Ten square feet of carpet will cover the floor of a room 10 feet by 10 feet.   30._____

## KEY (CORRECT ANSWERS)

| | | | |
|---|---|---|---|
| 1. | F | 16. | T |
| 2. | F | 17. | T |
| 3. | F | 18. | F |
| 4. | F | 19. | F |
| 5. | T | 20. | T |
| 6. | F | 21. | F |
| 7. | T | 22. | T |
| 8. | T | 23. | T |
| 9. | T | 24. | T |
| 10. | F | 25. | T |
| 11. | T | 26. | T |
| 12. | T | 27. | F |
| 13. | T | 28. | T |
| 14. | T | 29. | F |
| 15. | F | 30. | F |

## SOLUTIONS TO PROBLEMS

1. False. 48 ÷ 9 = 5 1/3 ≈ 5 miles, not 4 miles
2. False. (5)(10) = 50 min., not 1 hour
3. False. 1500 + (1/2)(1500) = 2250 men, not 2200 men
4. False. 186 ÷ 7 ≈ 27 summonses/hr., not 25 summonses/hr.
5. True. 186 - 100 = 86 summonses
6. False. (6)(50') = 300 ft., not 250 ft.
7. True. 2:18 reduces to 1:9
8. True. (200')-(36') = 7200 sq.ft. = 800 sq.yds. (1 sq.yd. = 9 sq.ft.)
9. True. 1 ton = 2000 lbs.
10. False. From 6 P.M. to 4 A.M. = 10 hrs., not 8 hrs.
11. True. (5 1/2')(1 1/2')(8') = 66 cu.ft.
12. True. 18 mi/hr is equivalent to 6 mi/g- hr = 6 mi/20 min
13. True. From 7/20/88 to 8/11/09 is 21 yrs. and 22 days
14. True. (231)(2.5) = 577.5 cu.in.
15. False. ($1.87)(100) = $187, not $18.70
16. True. Let x = wt. of load, 2x = wt. of truck. Then, 3x = 5400. Solving, x = 1800 lbs.
17. True. (8)(6) = 48 man-hours, so 48 ÷ 8 = 6 men
18. False. 1/2 mi. in 10 min. equals 3 mi/hr, not 15 mi/hr
19. False. 12 ÷ 3 = 4, and 1 1/2 ÷ 4 = 3/8 ton, not 1/2 ton
20. True. (6')(10')(6') = 360 cu.ft. = (6')(12')(5')
21. False. 2345 + 4483 = 6828, not 6882
22. True. (1/5)(295) = 59
23. True. 2876 - 1453 = 1423
24. True. (5)(15) = 75 cans
25. True. 245 ÷ 5 = 49 sections
26. True. (3)(4.5) = 13.5 man-hrs., so 13.5 ÷ 2 = 6.75 hrs.
27. False. 5 typists ÷ 4 boxes means each typist will have 4/5 box, not 1 box

28. True. Profit = $125 - $100 = $25, and $25 $125 = 20%

29. False. (1/2)(1/8) = 1/16, not 1/4

30. False. (10')(10') = 100 sq.ft., not 10 sq.ft.

# TEST 3

DIRECTIONS: Each question consists of a statement. You are to indicate whether the statement is TRUE (T) or FALSE (F). *PRINT THE LETTER OF THE CORRECT ANSWER IN THE SPACE AT THE RIGHT.*

1. If the medical examiner is expected to arrive an hour and fifteen minutes past 9:28 A.M. and he comes 12 minutes later than that, then it is 10:45 A.M. when he arrives.  1.____

2. A city hearse going at a rate of 44 miles an hour should cover 4 miles in 11 minutes.  2.____

3. If 8% of the alcohol in a container has evaporated, then 23/25ths of the original amount is still there.  3.____

4. If a mortuary caretaker works 7 hours each day for 46 days, the total number of hours he has worked in these 46 days is 322.  4.____

5. If a person's weight has gone down from 120 pounds to 105 pounds, his weight has gone down by 11%.  5.____

6. If Mortuary A has 26 bodies and Mortuary B has 2 more than twice as many as Mortuary A, then Mortuary B has 29 bodies.  6.____

7. Adding up these numbers: 2,693, 264, 1,701, and 849 gives a total of 4,507.  7.____

8. If bodies A and B together weigh 375 lbs. and body A alone weighs 187 pounds, then body B must weigh 188 pounds.  8.____

9. If 16 mortuaries are going to share equally 144 boxes of supplies, then each mortuary should get 9 boxes of supplies.  9.____

10. If eleven bodies are delivered to the mortuary the first day, 8 the second day, and 5 the third day, then the average number of bodies delivered per day for this period is 7.  10.____

11. If a temperature of 98.6 degrees is normal, then a temperature of 103.2 degrees is 4.6 degrees above normal.  11.____

12. If a hospital with a bed capacity of 2,100 beds reports that 87% of its beds are occupied, then the number of beds not occupied is 373.  12.____

13. It takes a hospital clerk 8 minutes to prepare an admission report on one patient. At this rate, it will take the hospital clerk 5 hours and 36 minutes to prepare the admission reports on 42 patients.  13.____

14. Three-fifths of the patients in Hospital X are males. If the total number of patients in Hospital X is 1,550, then the number of male patients is 930.  14.____

15. In a certain hospital, requests for laboratory examinations are made out in duplicate on a special laboratory request form. The laboratory request forms are bound in pads, each pad containing 80 forms. If 480 laboratory examinations were requested during the month of November, the number of pads used in November was 6 pads.  15.____

16. Of 1,376 apartments in a public housing project, 868 are three-room apartments. Therefore, the number of apartments in this project that are not three-room apartments is 508.  16.____

17. Attendant A is working twice as fast as Attendant B; therefore, in the same period of time, Attendant B does one-half the amount of work that Attendant A does.  17.____

18. An attendant has cleaned a wall 14 feet long and 7 feet high; he has, therefore, cleaned 108 square feet of wall surface.  18.____

19. An employee is paid $12.00 an hour for the first 40 hours that he works in one week and $18.00 an hour for every hour that he works over 40 hours in a week; therefore, if he works 50 hours in one week, he will be paid $660.  19.____

20. Each of six windows in a children's shelter measures 3 feet wide by 6 feet high; the total window space of these six windows is 126 square feet.  20.____

21. You are instructed to divide 1,092 paper towels equally among 14 people; therefore, you should give each person 78 towels.  21.____

22. If two wheels of unequal size are rolled the same distance across a floor, the smaller wheel will make less turns in this distance than the larger one.  22.____

23. An attendant who pays $9.13 each week for 49 weeks into a pension fund has, in this period of time, paid $447.37 into this pension fund.  23.____

24. In the course of his duties, an attendant must find the answer to 50 times 80. Adding up a column of fifty eighties will give the same answer as multiplying eighty by fifty.  24.____

25. An attendant gave these directions to a man who asked for a location in the city: *From 42nd Street and 8th Avenue, walk one block wests turn right and walk one blocks then turn left and walk half a block and you're at the place you're looking for.* Following these directions would place the man on 43rd Street.  25.____

## KEY (CORRECT ANSWERS)

1. F
2. F
3. T
4. T
5. T

6. F
7. F
8. T
9. T
10. F

11. T
12. F
13. T
14. T
15. F

16. T
17. T
18. F
19. T
20. F

21. T
22. F
23. T
24. T
25. T

# SOLUTIONS TO PROBLEMS

1. False. 9:28 A.M. + 1 hr. 15 min. + 12 rain. = 10:55 A.M., not 10:45 A.M.

2. False. 44 mi/hr = 4 mi. in $\frac{60}{11} = 5.\overline{45}$ min., not 11 min.

3. True. 100% - 8% = 92% = 23/25

4. True. (7)(46) = 322 hrs.

5. False. 120 - 105 = 15 lbs., and 15/120 = 12 1/2%, not 11%

6. False. 2 + (2)(26) = 54, not 29

7. False. 2693 + 264 + 1701 + 849 = 5507, not 4507

8. True. 375 - 187 = 188 lbs.

9. True. 144 16 = 9 boxes

10. False. (11+8+5) 3 = 8, not 7

11. True. 103.2° - 98.6° = 4.6°

12. False. 100% - 87% = 13%, and (13%)(2100) = 273, not 373

13. True. (8 min.)(42) = 336 min. = 5 hrs. and 36 min.

14. True. (3/5)(1550) = 930 male patients

15. False. Each exam requires 2 forms, so a pad of 80 forms is sufficient for 40 exams. Then, 480 ÷ 40 = 12 pads, not 6 pads

16. True. 1376 - 868 = 508 apartments

17. True. Since attendant A is twice as fast as attendant B, B's work = 1/2 the amount of A's work (in the same time)

18. False. (14')(7') = 98 sq.ft., not 108 sq.ft.

19. True. ($12)(40) + ($18)(10) = $660

20. False. (6)(3')(6') = 108 sq.ft., not 126 sq.ft.

21. True. 1092 ÷ 14 = 78 towels

22. False. A smaller wheel will actually make more turns in going the same distance as a larger wheel.

23. True. ($9.13)(49) = $447.37

24. True. Adding fifty 80's = (50)(80) = 4000

25. True. 42nd St. + 1 block north = 43rd St.

---

# DEPARTMENT OF SANITATION

## TABLE OF CONTENTS

| | Page |
|---|---|
| **ADMINISTRATION AND OPERATION** | 1 |
|   1. Office of the Director of Operations | 1 |
|   2. Bureau of Cleaning and Collection | 1 |
|   3. Bureau of Waste Disposal | 2 |
|   4. Bureau of Motor Equipment | 2 |
|   5. Bureau of Plant Maintenance | 2 |
|   6. Division of Safety | 3 |
|   7. Inspectional Force | 3 |
|   8. Sanitation Training Center | 3 |
|   9. Truck Measuring | 4 |
|   10. Operating Facilities Inspector | 4 |
| **SANITATION FACTS** | 5 |
|   1. The Assignment | 5 |
|   2. The Physical Job | 5 |
|   3. The People | 5 |
|   4. The Plan | 6 |
|   5. The Scope | 6 |
|   6. The Good Citizen | 6 |
|   7. The Good Merchant | 7 |
| **HEALTH CODE-SANITATION SECTION-EXCERPTS** | 8 |
|   1. Sidewalks and Streets | 8 |
|   2. Containers | 9 |
|   3. Lots, Yards and Areaways | 9 |
|   4. Miscellaneous | 10 |
|   5. Ice on Sidewalk | 10 |
| **FIVE RULES FOR A CLEAN CITY** | 10 |

# DEPARTMENT OF SANITATION

## ADMINISTRATION AND OPERATION

1. OFFICE OF THE DIRECTOR OF OPERATIONS

The Director of Operations supervises and coordinates the functions of the Bureaus of Cleaning and Collection, Waste Disposal, Motor Equipment, Plant Maintenance; the Division of Safety, the Training Center, the Operating Facilities Inspector's office and the work of the Inspectional Force – all of which perform duties assigned the Department by the City Charter.

These duties include: sweeping, cleaning, flushing, and sanding the city's streets; removal of ashes, sweepings, garbage, refuse, and rubbish; removal of ice and snow from the streets – plus the operation and maintenance of incinerators, landfills, marine transfer stations, and marine unloading plants for the disposal of municipal refuse.

With the aid of various bureau and division heads, the Director of Operations formulates basic plans, procedures and methods. He collaborates with the Director of Engineering in the development of long-range programs involving additions, changes, and improvements in Sanitation plant and equipment to achieve operating economies and improved service to the public.

2. BUREAU OF CLEANING AND COLLECTION

The Bureau of Cleaning and Collection, the largest operational unit of the Department, is headed by the Chief of Staff, who directs the work of nearly 1,000 officers and 9,000 sanitation men.

The Bureau, which has been likened to a municipal housekeeper for New York's 8,000,000 population and the multitudes that visit the city, is responsible for implementing two of the most important duties assigned the Department by the City Charter: the collection of refuse and the cleaning of streets. And seasonally, another vital responsibility is the removal of snow and ice.

Since the Bureau includes approximately 15,000 of the Department's 20,400 employees, who are spread over a wide area, a well-coordinated organizational plan is required. This is achieved via a close-knit system of headquarters (main office), borough, district and section commands.

For Sanitation purposes, the city's five boroughs are sub-divided into eight, each under the supervision of a Borough Superintendent. Manhattan, Brooklyn and Queens are divided into East and West commands. Orders originating with the Bureau head or higher are channeled through the office of the Chief of Staff to the Assistant and Deputy Chiefs of Staff, then to Borough Superintendents who in turn transmit them to the Department's 57 districts and 234 sections.

The average district is comprised of four sections and a garage, and is headed by a District Superintendent. A section, supervised by a foreman, conducts Department operations at the local level.

Sanitation districts vary greatly in size, population, and character. A heavily populated district might cover one square mile having 240,000 residents. Another district in an outlying part of the city may sprawl over 25 square miles and have a population of 46,000. Regardless of size of area, or density of population, or what type of problems face the District Superintendent, adjustments are made to meet specific local needs. Invariably, the end result has been sanitation services unmatched by any major city in the United States.

### 3. BUREAU OF WASTE DISPOSAL

The Bureau of Waste Disposal receives and finally disposes of all waste material collected by DS forces, by private carting companies, and by other authorized agencies. The bulk of this material is received from Department collection forces, but private carting companies play an increasingly important role in this operation.

A completely new item became part of the Bureau's activities when the Department took over the establishment and conduct of fills to receive demolition and construction waste. This was in line with the Mayor's decision to abolish all private landfills and give the Department the additional burden of more than a half-million cubic yards of construction waste per year. The three sections of this Bureau are the Division of Incinerator Operations, Division of Marine Operations, and Division of Fill Operations.

### 4. BUREAU OF MOTOR EQUIPMENT

The Bureau of Motor Equipment keeps the Department in motion – through the maintenance, repair and replacement of more than 4,000 pieces of automotive equipment.

An Assistant to the Commissioner directs a force of nearly 1,000 – including automobile mechanics, machinists, upholsterers, electricians, welders, sheet-metal workers, blacksmiths, battery and tire-repair men, supervisors, engineers and clerical help – in handling the upkeep of what is probably the world's largest municipal fleet of refuse collection trucks and street-cleaning and snow-fighting equipment.

### 5. BUREAU OF PLANT MAINTENANCE

This Bureau lends important aid to the big DS job by keeping in good repair the 350-odd city-owned and leased structures required to house the Department's many operations. These include garages, section stations, incinerators, marine transfer stations, landfills, marine unloading plants and other installations. In addition, the BPM repairs gasoline pumps, storage tanks, and similar items of Department plant.

A principal civil engineer directs the Bureau which is staffed by about 500 persons, among them planning and supervising engineers; craftsmen skilled in all the building trades; helpers, laborers, chauffeurs and clerks. Most of the Bureau's personnel work in (or operate out of) the BPM's Brooklyn headquarters or shops in Manhattan and the Bronx. For efficient management, the BPM is divided into two divisions – Structures and Painting.

## 6. DIVISION OF SAFETY

The director of safety and his 16-member staff work to protect Sanitation personnel from occupational hazards and the general public from incurring inconvenience or injury as a result of widespread DS operations.

Thus, accident and fire prevention, accident investigation, the instruction and testing of accident-prone personnel, the indoctrination of new employees, and the analysis of accident and injury data are major concerns of the Division.

## 7. INSPECTIONAL FORCE

The Department's law enforcement agency, insofar as concerns appropriate sections of the Sanitary and Administrative Codes, is the 500-man Inspectional Force.

Members of this unit, who derive their authority from the Police Commissioner, issued approximately 100,000 citations to Magistrates' Courts. As in previous years, the major cause of summons issuance involved the manner in which household refuse was put out for DS collection. A complete summary of the unit's enforcement work would show that it is a busy and effective force.

Under the supervision of a Captain-in-charge, the Inspectional Force performs its function largely via daily patrols which cover the whole city. The unit is divided into 16 divisions, each of which is supervised by a sergeant, and each borough (except Staten Island) is under the direction of a lieutenant.

## 8. SANITATION TRAINING CENTER

The Sanitation Training Center is at once a basic training facility for recruits, and a source of post-graduate refresher instruction for employees seeking advancement or specialized instruction for new or specific job purposes.

New employees are indoctrinated with the plan, scope and problems of New York's sanitation operation; they are told how to perform various jobs to which they will be assigned, and given complete orientation as to their privileges and obligations as members of the Department.

Older employees receive opportunities to attend appropriate in-service training courses when upcoming civil service examinations offer career opportunities.

## 9. TRUCK MEASURING

The primary job of the Truck Measuring unit is checking the cubic capacities of various types of privately owned vehicles which are engaged, or licensed, by the city. These include trucks of private cartmen licensed to haul refuse and trade waste, and those hired or contracted by the Department during snow emergencies.

This constant activity of the TM unit is to assure compliance with refuse-hauling regulations and to assure the city of receiving full value when it pays for hauling services rendered, when truckers remit dumping fees based on volumetric capacity, or when permits are granted in accordance with the rated capacity of privately owned trucks.

## 10. OPERATING FACILITIES INSPECTOR

The functions of the Operating Facilities Inspector, whose office is under the jurisdiction of the Director of Operations, are largely in the location and inspection of premises to be leased by the Department as potential housing for section stations, garages, shops, and other installations.

As the Department's real estate agent, the OFI maintains close liaison with the Bureau of Real Estate, the Department of Water Supply, Gas and Electricity, the Comptroller's Office, and other city agencies.

# SANITATION FACTS

INTRODUCTION

Ever since people began living in cities, they have had the problem of waste disposal – the removal of garbage, rubbish, and litter.

As cities have grown, so has the problem. Today in New York City, we have the biggest municipal housekeeping job of all. Here, some 8,000,000 people, plus millions of visitors, in addition to commerce and industry, annually produce about 10,000,000 tons of refuse.

Obviously each New York householder cannot safely and properly dispose of his portion of this waste. Nor can he be expected to sweep streets or clean them of snow. So New York City – or any city – must have a Sanitation Department.

Many different agencies have handled New York's sanitation job since colonial times, when pigs were allowed to roam the streets to eat up waste matter carelessly thrown there. In 1930, however, a citywide Sanitation Department was created, which has grown into what we know today as a 20,000-employee organization with an enormous budget – more than it costs to run the United Nations.

1. THE ASSIGNMENT

The City Charter assigns to the Department of Sanitation these duties:
- The sweeping, cleaning, flushing and sanding of the city's streets.
- The removal of ashes, sweepings, garbage, refuse rubbish, etc.
- The operation and maintenance of incinerators, landfills and marine transfer stations for the disposal of municipal waste.

2. THE PHYSICAL JOB

It is the DAILY task of the Department to clean 4,500 miles of paved streets; to collect and dispose of 3,000 truckloads of about 9,000 tons of refuse; to operate and maintain more than 4,000 pieces of motorized equipment – including 1,800 trucks on the streets ever day – and hundreds of pieces of snow-removal and waste-disposal equipment. At present the Department has 12 incinerators, nine landfills, 11 marine transfer stations (waterfront dumps) and two barge-unloading plants, between which shuttle units of the Sanitation "Navy" – four tugboats and 42 barges. Besides its Manhattan headquarters, the Department has 350 city-owned and leased premises in which are housed incinerators, garages, section-stations shops and other essential operations.

3. THE PEOPLE

Of our 20,000 employees, 15,000 are in the Bureau of Cleaning and Collection. Their biggest job is picking up (annually) about 10,000,000 tons of refuse – the DS share of the city's total discard. Some 4,000 people staff the Bureau of Waste Disposal, which handles DS-collected material and trade waste collected by private cartmen. Most employees hold the civil service title of sanitation man. There are 135 other titles and ranks.

## 4. THE PLAN

The city is divided into eight boroughs, subdivided into 57 districts and 234 section-stations for Sanitation purposes. Population of a DS district ranges from 50,000 to 240,000. A district ranges from one square mile in a crowded residential area to 25 square miles in less populated parts of the city.

After New York's refuse has been collected, either daily or thrice weekly, something must be done with it. Since dumping refuse at sea was stopped in 1934, there remain two chief means of disposal: (1) burning in incinerators, or (2) burying in carefully engineered land-reclamation projects.

Landfills receive incinerator residue (ashes) and other waste which is usually trucked there. The refuse is disinfected, compacted by bulldozers, graded, and covered with a thick layer of clean fill. When the work has been completed, formerly worthless land is transformed into parks or valuable tax-bearing property.

New incinerators, which cost about $6,500,000 each, can process up to 1,000 tons of refuse a day. Furnaces burn at 1,500-2,500 degrees Fahrenheit – 5 days a week, 24 hours a day.

## 5. THE SCOPE

The enormous quantity of refuse handled by the Sanitation Department is hard to picture. It may help to consider that a year's accumulation would fill the Empire State Building 15 times, or form a mile-high mountain on the playing field at Shea Stadium.

## 6. THE GOOD CITIZEN

You can be a good citizen – by helping the Department of Sanitation and the Citizens Committee to keep New York City clean. The law says you must help by observing the Health Code, which requires the following:

- Sidewalks must be kept swept at all times.
- Sweepings must be put into covered metal containers, not into DS litter baskets, which are for pedestrians' light litter only.
- DS litter baskets must be used – and properly.
- Dirt or litter must not be swept into the street at any hour.
- Snow must be cleared from sidewalks promptly.
- Garbage must be put out for collection at the proper time, and cans removed immediately after emptying.
- Never throw or dump paper, junk, debris or garbage on sidewalks, streets, areaways, courts, yards and vacant lots.
- Dogs must be controlled so as not to commit any nuisance on sidewalks or any other public place, except gutters.

Your cooperation will be appreciated. It is much easier to follow the Health Code than to receive penalties.

## 7. THE GOOD MERCHANT

To help you cooperate fully in the clean-city program, the Sanitary Code of the City of New York requires:
1) That sidewalks be kept swept at all times.
2) That there be no sweeping into the street at any hour.
3) That sweepings be put in refuse containers – not in DS litter baskets.
4) That sidewalks be kept free of snow and ice.
5) That metal containers with tight-fitting covers be used for refuse.
6) That excess materials (paper, cardboard, rags, etc.) be secured, bundled and tied.
7) That containers and bundled material be kept within building line until collection time, and containers removed from sidewalks immediately after being emptied.
8) That containers and excess materials be kept off sidewalks on Sundays and holidays.

These requirements are essential to the welfare and well being of all citizens. It is much easier to follow the Code provisions than to be subject to penalties. Sanitation patrolmen stationed in your area will be glad to answer any questions.

# HEALTH CODE-SANITATION SECTION-EXCERPTS

INTRODUCTION

In 1959 what was formerly the Sanitary Code became the new, revised Health Code of the City of New York. Its purpose is to safeguard the health and well being of all citizens.

This digest, which has been prepared in cooperation with the Department of Sanitation, lists provisions of the Health Code that apply specifically to littering and to other violations of the laws governing community cleanliness.

These violations are subject to summonses to Magistrates' Courts, with fines up to $25. In flagrant cases the fines can be as high as $500, a year in prison, or both.

No infractions need to happen. It is hoped, therefore, that through increased public awareness of the laws, citizens – acting in their OWN interests – will voluntarily cooperate to make and keep our city clean.

Such cooperation is a moral obligation in any community. In many, including New York City, the law requires it – and backs its demands with enforcement.

A cleaner New York is up to all of us. Each individual can help by obeying the Health Code.

1. SIDEWALKS AND STREETS

Dirty Sidewalks (Sec. 153.19): Sidewalks must be kept clean at all times by those whose properties face on them.

Sweep-out (Sec. 153.01): Dirt and litter must not be swept from the sidewalk into the gutter and street at any time. Sidewalk sweepings must be put into suitable garbage cans for pick-up by the Sanitation Department or by private collection service.

Throwout or Dumping (Sec. 153.01): No litter, garbage, cans, ashes, rubbish or broken glass may be thrown or dumped onto sidewalks, streets, areaways, yards or lots. Throwing things out of windows is included in this violation.

Sidewalk Obstruction (Sec.153.19): No refuse or discarded objects may be put on the sidewalk where they can obstruct or interfere with passage while such waste is awaiting collection by Sanitation or private service.

Littering: Littering is further prohibited by the City's Administrative Code, Section 755 (3)-2.1, as follows:
No person shall litter, sweep, throw or cast, or direct or permit any servant, agent, employee or other person under his control to litter, sweep, throw or cast any ashes, garbage, paper, dust or other rubbish or refuse into any public street or place, vacant lot, air shaft, areaway, backyard or court.

Dogs: Dog Nuisances (Sec. 161.03); Unleashed (Sec. 161.05)

Dogs are to be controlled so that they do not commit any nuisance on sidewalks. They must be leashed and walked in the gutter.

## 2. CONTAINERS (Sec. 131.11)

Improper use of DS Litter Baskets: Litter baskets are designed for the use of passing pedestrians. They are intended as containers for scrap paper, newspapers, candy wrappers, cigarette packages, fruit skins and similar light refuse.

They are NOT intended for household refuse or for the use of nearby property owners, tenants or storekeepers, who are required by law to provide their own containers.

Material Put Out for Collection: Containers for garbage, refuse and ashes must be kept within the building or in rear of premises until time for removal. They then must be placed in front of building or on sidewalk close to the building.

Loose Rubbish: All newspapers, loose paper, rubbish and rags must be tied securely before being put out for collection as excess rubbish.

Insufficient Containers: Each location must have enough leak-proof garbage cans for 60 hours accumulation so that they will not be overloaded at any time.

Broken Containers: All garbage cans must be in good repair. Broken cans which may leak, permit litter to escape, or injure people handling them must be replaced.

Uncovered Containers: Garbage cans must be covered at all times with tight-fitting covers.

Mixed Material: Separate cans must be used for garbage and ashes. This helps disposal by the Department of Sanitation.

Into garbage cans should go all perishable material such as meat, fat, bones, fish, fruit, and vegetables. Into ash cans should go all unburnable material such as ashes, bottles, cans, crockery, glass, and sweepings.

## 3. LOTS, YARDS AND AREAWAYS

Backyards and Areaways (Sec. 153.19): Owners, superintendents, tenants or occupants are responsible for the cleanliness of backyards, courtyards and areaways of the premises.

Dirty Lots (Sec. 153.19): An owner, lessee or manager of a vacant lot is responsible for its cleanliness and must see that there is no accumulation of rubbish, water or offensive material thereon.

## 4. MISCELLANEOUS

Noxious Liquids (Sec. 153.09): No swill, brine, offensive animal matter or any odious or noxious liquids must be allowed to run or fall on any street, nor may they be placed there.

Dust Flying (Sec. 153.03): No mop may be shaken nor carpet beaten so that litter or dust is created.

No reasonable precautions must be taken to prevent the scattering or blowing about of lime, ashes, coal, sand, hair, feathers or similar substances likely to be blown by the wind.

Interfering with DS Work (Sec. 153.13): A Sanitation employee must not be interfered with in sweeping or cleaning a street or in the removal of ashes, garbage, rubbish, snow or ice.

Spilling from Truck (Sec. 153.11): No person in control of a vehicle shall permit any litter or other material to scatter, drop or spill from such vehicle.

Distributing Circulars (Sec. 153.17): It is illegal to distribute commercial advertising circulars except through the United States Mail. Among other things, this applies to distribution to pedestrians and to attaching such circulars to automobiles.

## 5. ICE ON SIDEWALK

Under Section 755(3)-2.0a, every owner, lessee, tenant, occupant or other person having charge of any lot or building shall, within four hours after snow has ceased to fall or within four hours after 7 a.m. if snow has ceased to fall after 9 p.m. the previous evening, clean such snow or ice from the sidewalk.

Under Section 755(3)-2.0b, in the event snow or ice becomes frozen so hard it is unlikely that it can be removed, the sidewalk is to be strewn with ashes, sand, sawdust or similar suitable material. (The same above-mentioned four-hour time limit applies here.) The sidewalk is to be thoroughly cleaned as soon thereafter as the weather permits.

FIVE RULES FOR A CLEAN CITY
1. Use litter baskets.
2. Put all garbage INSIDE garbage cans.
3. Keep sidewalks clean – Put sweepings in your trash cans.
4. Never put trash in vacant lots.
5. Curb your dog.

www.ingramcontent.com/pod-product-compliance
Lightning Source LLC
Chambersburg PA
CBHW082040300426
44117CB00015B/2557